THE ADVANCED CREATIVE OJO BOOK

by

Diane Thomas

Copyright © 1975 by Diane Thomas
Hunter Publishing Company
P.O. Box 9533
Phoenix, Arizona 85068
Phone 602-944-1022

LIBRARY OF CONGRESS
CATALOG CARD NO. 75-44655
ISBN #0-918126-01-0

TABLE OF CONTENTS

**ALL OJOS ARE COLOR ILLUSTRATED ON
PAGES 26-27 OR ON BACK COVER**

INTRODUCTION TO OJOS

(God's Eye)

These colorful talismans, pronounced OHO-DAY-DEEOS, were originally made in North America by the Pueblo and Mexican Indians. But they are much older than this, for they appear in the tombs of ancient Egyptian rulers, wound of fibers from the Nile river banks. In fact, an eye appears on the pyramid of the U. S. one dollar bill. On a recent trip to Northern Europe, the author found 200 year old ojos in the museums of Scandinavia, modern day ojos in Poland, ojo jewelry in the marketplaces of Finland. No one is sure when the first ojo was woven of simple sticks plucked from a bush or shrub, and wound with river rushes or vines, but even before Christianity man has used the shape of the cross to invoke protection.

The early Indians, whose ancestors are believed to have come from Egypt, were perhaps only renewing an ancient belief when they sought good health, good crops, good fortune from an ojo made to be displayed on the walls of their cave dwellings. Today the modern Indians still perpetuate the custom of asking for protection from a being more powerful than their chiefs.

Although the making of ojos has become an art form, refined to fit the sophisticated homes of today, the simple beauty of their execution has persisted. They may be made of nylon and metallic threads rather than growing vines, but their meaning is the same — May the Eye of God be on you, and bring peace, plenty and happiness to your household.

There is no more sincere way to say "I wish you well" than to make a gift of an ojo; and no better way to pay homage to ancient beliefs than to make an ojo for your own home.

If you are not thoroughly familiar with the basic techniques of ojo making, **The Creative Ojo Book,** a beginner's manual, gives a realistic grounding in all ojo construction, with simple and intermediate projects carefull diagrammed.

TERMINOLOGY

Attaching yarn: Unless otherwise directed, yarn is always glued on back of ojo arm with cut end toward left and ball of yarn toward right. It is then brought to front by flipping ojo frame to the left.

Eye or top wrap: This means a simple wrap covering each stick in rotation counterclockwise, working from the front of the ojo at all times. When used as the start of the ojo, it forms the eye at the cross of the sticks. Used as the ojo progresses, it is known as the top wrap. (see **Diagram A**)

Double eye wrap: Occasionally an ojo is designed to be hung as a mobile, or placed so it can be viewed from both sides, as in a room divider. Then it is necessary to wrap both sides at the same time. This is done by passing over 2 sticks, returning to starting point, then passing over the next stick in rotation as in the regular eye wrap. This is repeated until the eye is the desired size. (see **Diagram B**)

Oblong eye: When sticks are glued at any angle other than 90°, a square eye will not result. An oblong eye is wrapped by crossing between two sticks to cover center then wrapping as directed. With a two stick ojo, the eye will be wrapped on each arm. With a three (or more) stick ojo, directions will indicate how to wrap. Resulting eye, in any case, will be oblong in shape.

Back wrap: The method for back wrapping is the same as top wrapping only the back wrap is done on the back side of the ojo forming a recessed framing when viewed from the front side.

Changing from top (or back) wrap to back (or top) wrap: There is no need to glue off when changing from one wrap to another. Simply give the yarn an extra half twirl around the stick to bring it up on the opposite side and start wrapping from other side of ojo. Be sure to complete a round before changing.

Wing wrap: The decorative arrow effect of this wrap adds much to the ojo design. It is done by wrapping opposing arms (e. g. 1 and 3, 2 and 4, 5 and 7, etc.) with a top wrap while passing under the other arms. In doing the wing wrap, the long strands must lie smoothly on the back of the ojo to produce an even "mitering" of the yarn on the wings. When trimming a wing wrap, the outline wraps must be applied to each set of wing wraps before moving on to the new arms for the next wing wrap. The wing wrap represents the Indian arrows, used in ojos as a protection from evil. (see **Diagram C**)

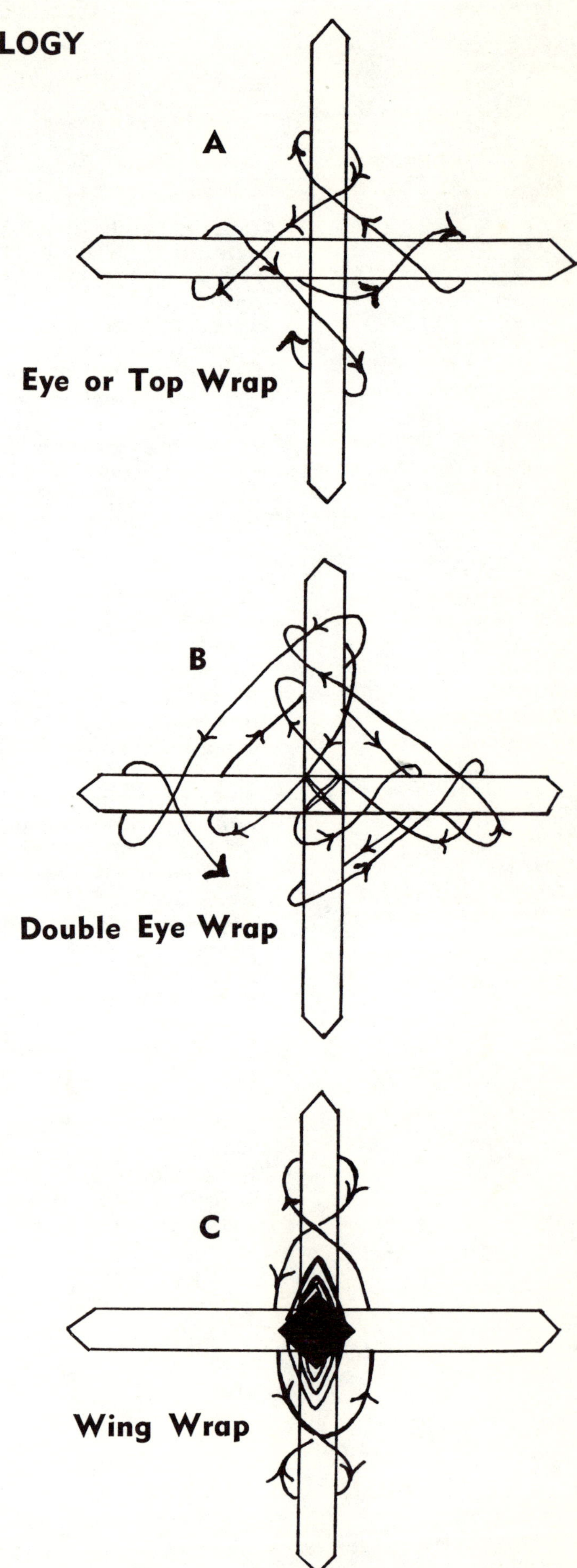

TERMINOLOGY (Cont.)

SIMPLE FINGER KNOT: A simple knotting of two threads together as in knotting ends of sewing thread.

LARKSHEAD KNOT: Drawing the ends through a hairpin loop to fasten over a stick or wire. See diagram in NIGHT OWL MACRAME.

SPIDER WRAP: A two round top wrap used to fill spaces in a 3 stick ojo, or to top-accent a 4 or 6 stick ojo by a spidery skipping of every other stick in wrapping.

STAR WRAP: This is done by top wrapping every 2nd arm in an 8 arm ojo for a desired number of rounds, always passing under the skipped arm or arms. Then attach yarn to next arm in sequence and repeat alternating wrap.

EXTEND WRAP: This is used to open spaces in the ojo for a more lacey effect. The yarn is wound smoothly around the sticks, one at a time, until the covering is the length desired. A variation of this is to connect the extend wraps. Instead of gluing off each time, the yarn is carried from the end of the extend wrap on one arm to the beginning of the next. To be effective, the extend wrap in this case must be at least 1½" down the stick before moving on to next arm.

FIGURE 8 WRAP: This wrap is worked on only 2 arms at a time. The yarn is wound in a figure 8 pattern over the top of the first arm, crossed between the first and second arm and wound from behind the second arm. (See Diagram D)

D 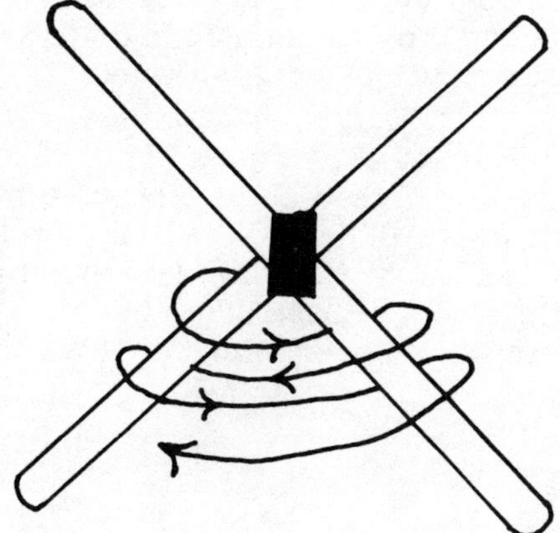

FIGURE 8 WRAP

SPACE WRAP: When doing a space wrap, as in **TREE** or **KITE** shapes, the yarn is wrapped two or more times around an arm instead of the usual once. Anytime the yarn is "bunching" on an arm, an extra wrap may be taken to help it lie flat.

CANDY TWIST: A very effective trim which can be used to outline wing wraps, define changes of color, or trim the outer edges of an ojo is obtained by tightly twisting two colors together as you do either a top or back wrap. Tension must be snug on this wrap since the two strands of yarn may tend to "roll" on previous wrap. When doing the twisted wraps, premeasure the number of rounds you intend to make, add an extra 6" for each round, and cut yarn to avoid tangling.

CHEVRON TWIST: This is a variation of the candy twist and is accomplished by doing the candy twist for one round, gluing securely, then reversing the twist by "spinning", the two yarns in the opposite direction through your fingers as you top or back wrap. A little practice will enable you to make a chevron design as the two twists lie together.

TWIRLING: Yarn may be wound by the "throw" or "twirling" method. Twirling is more desirable. Instead of looping the yarn around each arm, hold each arm in succession in left hand, yarn in right, spin ojo completely around letting yarn wind around arm required number of turns. Keeping yarn in right hand, turn ojo ¼ turn to right, change hand from previous arm to new arm and repeat spin.

NOTCHING: Lay the sticks on top of each other and carefully mark for notching. Use a small hacksaw to start cut, then either with an X-Acto knife or small chisel, very carefully cut out to half the depth of the wood. Notch each piece the same, checking for fit.

TENSION: There is no way to gauge perfect tension except to try a few rounds. Too tight tension will cause the sticks to break; too loose tension will make an unsightly ojo. Doing is the way of learning.

BASIC OJO CROSS: A basic ojo reference in this book means a simple 90º angle cross with the two sticks being notched in the center and each arm being of equal length.

SHIELD FRAME: This is any ojo frame made of 3 sticks glued together at center, whether in a 45º or 60º pattern.

ADVANCED TERMINOLOGY

VERTICAL DIAMOND WRAP: A vertical design is obtained by wrapping two turns around arms 1 and 3 and one around arms 2 and 4. This will elongate the wrappings in a vertical plane.

VERTICAL DIAMOND SPACE WRAP: When a sharper vertical deliniation is required, three turns are taken around arms 1 and 3, and one turn around arms 2 and 4.

HORIZONTAL DIAMOND WRAP: A horizontal design is obtained by wrapping two turns around arms 2 and 4 and one around arms 1 and 3. This elongates the yarn in a horizontal plane.

HORIZONTAL DIAMOND SPACE WRAP: When a faster "travel" along the horizontal arms is required, three turns are taken along arms 2 and 4, and one turn around arms 1 and 3.

HEXAGON EYE: When a shield frame of 3 sticks is wound at one time, each arm in rotation, a hexagon eye results. In this case, no skipping of sticks is done, and eye must be started by crossing in an X pattern for 2 or 3 times before wrapping each stick. This is also called a **6 POINT EYE.**

HALF-EYE: When winding a wall tree wrap, the ojo eye will only be on 3 of the 4 arms, thus a half eye will result. The measuring is the same as a regular eye — along the side.

FLOWER EYE: On an 8 arm ojo (shield frame), attach yarn on arm 8, wind over 3 arms (arm 2, counting original arm 8 as one arm), back around arm 1, over 3 arms (arm 3), back around arm 2, over 3 arms (arm 4) back around arm 3, over arm 5, back around arm 4, over arm 6, back around arm 5, over arm 7, back around arm 6, over arm 8, back around arm 7, over arm 1, back around arm 8. TO MEASURE: measure across as in top wrap.

SPECTRUM WRAP: (Used on a 12 arm ojo). Color A is glued on designated arm with cut end to left when facing back of ojo. Color B is glued directly beneath as closely as possible with cut end to right. Both colors are worked at once, first the color A, then color B. This wrap is used on a 12 stick ojo. With color A, wrap over arm 1, under and around arm 5, over and around arm 9, under and around arm 2, over and around arm 6, under and around arm 10, over and around arm 3, under and around arm 7, over and around arm 11, under and around arm 4, over and around arm 8, under and around arm 12, over and around arm 1.

With color B, under and around arm 1, over and around arm 5, under and around arm 9, over and around arm 2, under and around arm 6, over and around arm 10, under and around arm 3, over and around arm 7, under and around arm 11, over and around arm 4, under and around arm 8, over and around arm 12, under and around arm 1. Be careful each time you return to arm 1 to lock colors together with a twist on the back side.

WALL TREE WRAP: A wrapping done on only 3 of the 4 arms of an ojo so wrapping is all on one side. It is done by attaching yarn on arm 2, wrapping over arm 2, over arm 3, over arm 4 with 1½ turns, back across face of ojo to arm 3, over arm 2 with 1½ turns and back across face to arm 3, etc. See diagram for VIKING SHIELD.

DOUBLE TREE WRAP: Glue yarn behind arm 2. Top wrap over arm 2, over arm 3, over arm 4 with 1½ turns. This brings ojo around to back side facing you. Go over arm 3 and over arm 2 with 1½ turns. Right side is now facing you. Repeat this, wrapping only arms 2 to 3 to 4, back to 3 to 2, back to 3, etc. The result will be a half-eye (since arm 1 is not wound), which is measured along the side as in a regular eye. When gluing off or on, always complete front and back wrap; e.g., 3 rounds will then be 3 strands of yarn on front side and 3 on back. End on arm 2.

TRIPLE STAR WRAP: Used on a 12, 18 or 24 arm shield ojo. Yarn is wound over one arm, skip two arms, wind over 3rd arm until returning to starting arm. Yarn is then glued on next sequential arm, wound over that arm, next two arms skipped, over next arm, to starting point. Pattern is repeated until all arms have been wound.

DOUBLE WRAP: Yarn is wound over two sequential arms twice, then over second arm. e.g. Glue on arm 1, wrap over arms 1 and 2, back around arms 1 and 2, then around arm 2; over arms 2 and 3, back around arms 2 and 3 and around arm 3, etc., winding on both sides of ojo at once.

DOUBLE COLOR WRAP: Two yarns are worked at same time in reverse windings. Attach color 1 on any designated arm in a basic 4 arm ojo with color 2 directly beneath but coming from opposite direction. With 1st color, wind over 1st arm, under and around 2nd, over and around 3rd and under and around 4th, returning to starting arm. With 2nd color, twisting threads to "lock" color 1, wind from under 1st arm, over and around 2nd, under and around 3rd, over and around 4th and return to start. Repeat number of times directed.

DOUBLE SHIELD WRAP: This is an advanced version of double color wrap, used on ojos of more than 4 arms. See diagram for TABLE OJO. **NOTE:** In any double wrap, it is necessary to make the last round by taking a half turn to bring ojo to back side, then do a simple top wrap on all arms to complete number of rounds to match back and front.

RELEVANT FACTS

Sticks Used: Most ojos in this book are made on wood sticks, not dowels. In using dowels, glue must be applied to back of sticks while wrapping. This is not required when using squarish sticks. The lumber is clear Douglas fir, expensive but strong. The best way to obtain these sticks is to order two 1" x 6" boards, 6' long milled into wide sticks on one board and narrow on the other. That will give you enough lumber to make many ojos and the milling charge, while high, will be more economical than charged for a single board. Practice ojos may be made on scrap lumber, but this is not advised for making those you want to keep or give for gifts.

Stick Sizes: Directions call for either narrow or wide sticks. The narrow sticks are milled to ¼" x ⅜". The wide sticks are milled to ¾" x ⅜". A little planning before cutting up for ojo projects will enable you to get the most out of each length. **ANY OJO OVER 24" IN STICK LENGTH SHOULD BE MADE OF WIDE PIECES.**

Glue Used: Sticks should be glued together with any white household glue. Extra glue may be used to fill in notches that do not fit perfectly, or wood putty may be used. The glue used in the wrapping should be a flexible type such as Tacky.

MEASUREMENTS

THE EYE: To measure the eye, place ruler along the side of the eye, not across the center. In measuring an oblong eye, measure the long side.

THE WING: To measure the wing, place ruler along the center herringbone of the wing, measuring from the start to the point.

FLAT WRAPS: To measure either top or back wraps, measure across the threads at right angles.

STARTING AND STOPPING

Unless otherwise directed, winding material is always glued on the back side of the ojo. Starting point is usually arm 1. Threads are **never** tied off, but are glued neatly. When changing colors, the old and new ends are pushed snugly together to avoid unwanted spacing. When wrapping dimensionals, be sure the new yarn starts in the same direction as the old finished, treating the new thread as a continuation of the old.

When adding a new color to one already being worked to make a twist wrap, it will be easier to put glue on arm, then slip new color under continuing color and press down on both yarns. Let it dry before proceeding with twist wrap.

Check carefully whenever changing colors frequently to be sure the starting and stopping is not spacing out your yarns. If the constant gluing off and on is making you go down one arm faster than you should, try tightly twisting the end to be glued to make it as small as possible.

HANGING

With a piece of matching thread, pick a place in the wrapping about 3" down the arm. Tie in snugly with a double square knot. (Go over thread twice before pulling down). Then tie loop with single finger knot, just as you knot sewing thread.

HANGING MOBILES

When hanging mobiles, you may want to have them swing more freely than can be enjoyed with a simple loop hanging. In this case, attach a very small swivel, obtainable in any hardware store and most hobby shops, to the top of the ojo. It will then turn freely in any air current.

IMAGINATION USED:

Don't feel you can use only one ojo on a wall. Try making an arrangement as you would with pictures, hanging a grouping of them. You can even mix them up in color in a grouping, as you would with paintings. The groupings are especially attractive with a mixture of mini and larger ojos hung together. (See WALL HANGING)

MAKING ENDS NEAT

Arrowing: Make an arrow-shaped template from a piece of stiff material, such as plastic from the cover of a stationery box. Center the point carefully on sticks and cut with a small saw.

Beveling: The ends of your sticks may be beveled by either drawing them toward you, one side at a time, on rough sandpaper, or by holding against a grinding wheel.

Painting: Sticks may be painted with water-based or oil-based paint. They may also be stained with wood stains. It is better to paint sticks before wrapping, but they can be colored later by painting before the last few rounds of wrapping.

Pompons: One of the quickest and easiest trims for ojos is pompons. Used on the hanging arm, they cover the hanging loop. Made of strands of the colors used in the ojo, they tend to tie the whole design together. The best way to make even pompons is to use one of the kits available in knitting shops for less than $2, with several size templates in the kit.

Tasseled Pompon: Make pompon in usual fashion. Cut 4 strands of yarn 12" long. Before tying center thread of pompon tight, pull extra strands of yarn through to center, allowing ends to dangle freely. Complete pompon fastening.
Note: To the Indians, the pompon represents a puffy cloud, symbol of the gentle life-giving rains.

Flat Pompons: In trimming the top side of a mobile ojo, or sometimes on a wall-hanging ojo, a full rounded pompon is not desired. In this case, a flat pompon is made by using only ⅔ the usual amount of yarn pieces and allowing the pompon to flatten out when tied in place.

Arrowheads: These effective trims are available at most stores carrying Indian items or souvenir items. Glued to stick ends, or even on eye, they give a true Indian appearance to your ojo.

Shrink Art: A simple trim for special theme ojos can be made using the quick method of Shrink Art plastic on patterns in children's books, greeting cards, craft books, etc. To attach to the ojo, use a small piece of wood to give dimension and attach by gluing Shrink Art to wood piece, then glue to ojo.

Beadwork: Most Indian stores and souvenir shops carry some beadwork on thongs for wear around neck, etc. These can be detached and used to trim the ojo eye or the stick ends. Be careful not to cut any threads that may hold beads to backing. Attach with glue.

French Tassels: While the regular cardboard wound tassel can be used, the French tassel is far more attractive and is easily made. Wind the regular tassel on a piece of cardboard, allowing 1½ inches more than the desired length, (e.g. if you want a tassel which measures 6", cut the cardboard 7½" long). Tie at the top in the usual fashion, and tie around top as though making a simple tassel. Then flip tassel upside down, holding by tied part. Tie again, this time below the first tie. Carefully pull up two strands of yarn from opposite sides for attaching to ojo.

Shooting Tassels: Start by making a regular French tassel around cardboard pattern and tying the threads together at the top. Then dipping end of ojo arm ¼" into glue, arrange tassel pieces around stick end pointing **TOWARD** the eye of the ojo. Tie firmly just above glue line. Let dry thoroughly. Then bring ends back toward end of stick and tie firmly just below the stick end. (Shooting tassels should be short enough to stand out and not droop.)

Feathers: One of the more traditional trims for ojos is the use of feathers. They can be used singly or in groups at the ends of the sticks. To apply, wrap stick with same wool as last top or back wrap, glue feathers about ½ inch back on sticks, and rewrap with same wool to cover feather spine.

Feather Tassels: Another use of feathers is to make feather tassels. Attach a cluster of 4 or 5 small feathers to a piece of leather thong by knotting into end. With wool, wrap top of feathers covering knot. String several colored wooden beads on thong. With wool, cover balance of thong and leave end for tying to ojo arm.

Cockaded Tassel: A different version of the shooting tassel is made by cutting the tassel pieces an extra ½" in length, tying as directed for shooting tassel, then combing with a wire pet brush, or similar stiff bristled brush while lying on a flat surface. Be careful not to pull out too much of the yarn fibre. Then while still lying flat, trim into an arc shape with the center left the highest point. NOTE: Some yarns will not brush out; try a few pieces before making tassel.

Beaded Ends: An inexpensive and effective trimming for shield and other multi-arm ojos is the use of a dough-like medium that can be baked to resemble ceramic after painting. One such product is Sculpey. The advantage is the ability to make any dimension opening desired to fit on any size stick being used. After painting, these trims look very professional and cost only pennies. They may be painted with the same acrylic paints used on your sticks, to match or contrast, and the basic compounds are available in most craft shops. The dough can be shaped to your own design, and would be most effective on PINWHEEL or LIGHTNING SHIELD.

CENTER TRIMS

With more advanced ojo designing, it is often desirable to leave the centers unwound and trim by using related items to partially or completely cover the unwrapped center sticks.

Imagination can be used to provide many different center trims. The Hopi Indians use half heads of Kachina dolls. You can make a striking trim by designing a HOPI SUN GOD.

Buy a Prym metal button base available in any fabric store or notion department of a department store. Working with only the top section, spray with 3 separate coats of plastic spray. When thoroughly dry, paint button with white acrylic paint. Let dry. Then with a small brush and black acrylic paint, mark off with a half-way horizontal bar, and a half vertical bar as shown in diagram. Paint right quarter either blue or red, and left half either yellow or red. With black, mark off eyes and mouth as shown. Spray with plastic between each painting, and use two coats to finish.

Laying feathers on back section, wedging between metal "teeth", cover button circle completely. Arrange carefully and snap button top in place. (If feathers cannot be trimmed to thin enough quills to allow button to be snapped in place, feathers can be placed behind button top and glued in place, then whole assembly be glued to ojo by using a small circle of styrofoam to fasten button to ojo.)

Another attractive center trim can be a small sandpainting available in most Indian shops. In square or oblong shapes, they can be chosen to complement the shape of your ojo. If you wish to make your own sandpainting, many hobby stores have kits.

An unusual center trim can be such a simple thing as a cheap Indian drum, mini size, available in souvenir shops. Spray the drum with several coats of plastic spray to prevent tearing the fabric, then carefully saw the drum either in half, or the desired depth and apply to center of ojo with glue.

HOPI SUN GOD PATTERN

MAKING A TEMPLATE

To make anything other than a regular right-angle cross ojo frame, it is necessary to calculate angles very carefully. To do this, make a good template which can be used for all special ojos.

Using a piece of poster board or a letter-sized sheet of paper, draw a perfect circle. You many use a plate, pot lid or a compass. Find the center and mark with a small circle dot. Draw the vertical and horizontal lines which bisect the circle. These will be your guide lines for either vertical or horizontal base sticks, whenever called for.

With a protractor on the vertical line, mark for 30°, 45° and 60° angles. These are the ones you will usually use. Draw them in on the circle. If you wish, you may use different colored lines for each angle.

When notching angled sticks, always be sure to mark the center and place the mark on your template center. One caution, if you are making a 3-stick angled frame, such as **ROMAN CANDLE,** where the vertical stick is not marked in the center, but at a stated measurement up or down from the end, then place that marking, such as 5" up from bottom, on the center of the template when laying the crossed sticks on top for notching.

When placing the sticks, be sure to place the center of the stick on the line, not the edge of the stick. And when there is no vertical stick used, be careful to figure it as the angle cross. For example, when the directions say place the two sticks at 30° angle to the vertical, this means the sticks are laid on the 30° line even though no vertical stick will be used. Always notch and glue the angle sticks, then place on the vertical or horizontal stick and notch only the lower stick for the final gluing.

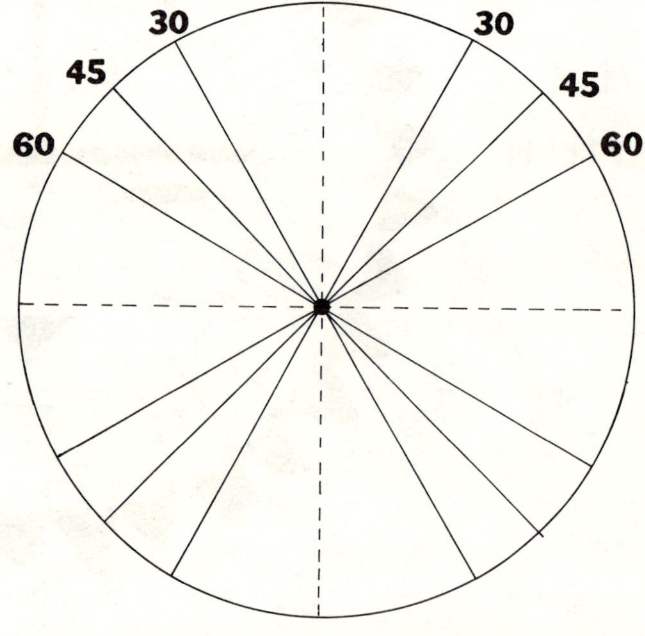

KUOPIO

This necklace is a copy of the ones for sale at the weekly outdoor market in Kuopio, Finland. There they are made of colored straw. This ojo can either be worn as a necklace or hung as a wall decoration in a small area.

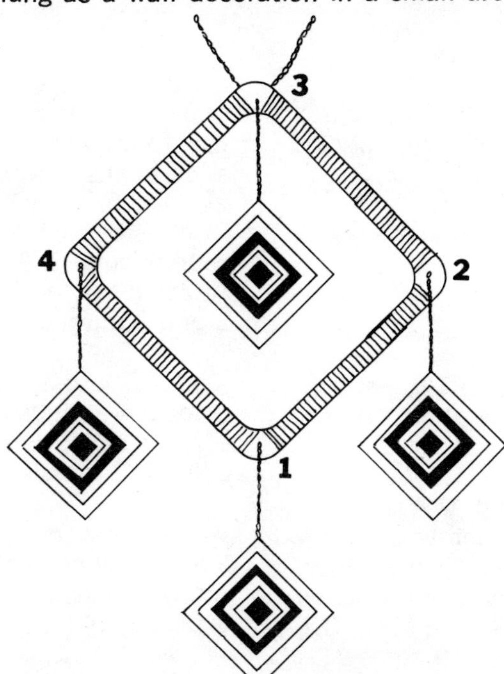

STICKS:
Four popsicle sticks, 4½" long (available in craft shops). Eight bamboo skewer pieces 2¾" long (available in Oriental gift shops), or you may use the smallest size dowel sticks.

GLUING:
Glue skewer pieces into four basic ojos. Glue popsicle sticks into a square. Paint bright blue.

PROCEDURE:
Yarn used is one-ply Persian so you must separate the yarn into one and two strands.

Using one strand pieces on mini ojo #1, * do ½" eye in color 1. Working all top wrap do ⅜" color 2. Do ⅜" in color 3. Finish out with color 4.

With colors 5, 6, 7, & 8, work second mini ojo from*.

With colors 9, 10, 11, & 12, work third mini ojo from*.

With colors 13, 14, 15, & 16, work fourth mini ojo from*.

On popsicle square, extend wrap each side with one strand as follows: Side one; ⅞" each of color 1, color 2, color 3, color 4. Side two; ⅞" each of color 5, color 6, color 7, color 8. Side three; ⅞" each of color 9, color 10, color 11, color 12. Side four; ⅞" each of color 13, color 14, color 15, color 16.

With 5/64" drill, make a hole in each corner of popsicle square.

With crochet hook #0, make a 1" chain of color 4 leaving 1½" ends. Make a 1½" chain each of colors 8, 12, and 16, leaving 1½" ends.

Using triangular jump rings, fasten top of 1½" chain threads to arms 1, 2, and 4. Fasten 1" chain thread to arm 3 with jump ring. Carefully glue other end of chain threads to arm 3 of mini ojos.

FINISHING:
Using double strands of colors 3, 11, and 15, knot ends together with simple finger knot. With simple braiding work the 3 colors for 30" and knot ends with simple finger knot. Slip behind ring in arm 3 of popsicle square. If ojo is to be hung on wall, a 2" braided loop may be substituted for neck chain.

COLOR CHART
1. Light green
2. Medium green
3. Bright green
4. Dark green
5. Yellow
6. Light orange
7. Medium orange
8. Dark orange
9. Light blue
10. Medium blue
11. Teal blue
12. Dark blue
13. Pink
14. Light rose
15. Medium rose
16. Dark rose

ROMAN CANDLE

This ojo is typical of the style made by the Huicol Indians of Mexico. It is easily adaptable to any size by simply adding longer sticks at the ends of the crosspiece. Yarn used is light weight sport.

STICKS:

Cut one 34" and one 28" narrow width. Using fireplace matches, cut seven 10" sticks and eighteen 2½" sticks.

NOTCHING:

Notch 34" stick at 8½" up, 17" up, 22" up, 28½" up and 32½" up.
Notch all 2½" sticks in center.

GLUING:

Step 1 — Notch one 10" stick in center and 1½" in from each end. Glue center notch on long stick at 8½" notch. Glue two 2½" sticks at end notches.

Step 2 — Notch 28" stick in center and 1½" in from each end. Glue two 2½" sticks at end notches. Notch four-10" sticks 1½" from each end. Using protractor, notch four-10" sticks at center to make 60 degree angles to 28" stick 6" from ends (See MAKING A TEMPLATE), glue in place and glue four 2½" sticks at end notches.

Step 3 — Glue one 2½" stick at 22" notch on long stick.

Step 4 — Notch the last two 10" sticks 1½" from each end, and at center at a 40 degree angle to the 28" stick. Adjust 28½" notch to fit and glue in place. Glue four-2½" sticks at end notches.

Step 5 — Glue last small stick at 32½" notch.

PROCEDURE:

Beginning at lower cross, make a ½" eye in color 1. With color 2 do 3 rounds, with color 3 do 3 rounds. Glue off. Matching both ends, do a ¼" eye in color 4, then 3 rounds color 5, 3 rounds in color 2 and 2 rounds color 6. Glue off.

At 17" cross, do a 1½" eye in color 7, then 4 rounds color 8, 4 rounds color 5, 4 rounds color 1 and 3 rounds color 4. Glue off.

COLOR CHART

1. Cerise
2. Orange
3. Green
4. Royal blue
5. Yellow
6. Purple
7. Black
8. Red
9. Peacock

On 28" cross stick, matching both ends on 10" sticks, make a shield eye ¾" with color 9. Then 4 rounds color 6, 4 rounds color 1 and 3 rounds color 3. At end of 28" stick, make matching eyes on small sticks with ½" eye in color 3, then 3 rounds color 8 and 3 rounds color 2. At ends of each 10" stick, do a ½" eye of color 9, then 3 rounds color 2, 3 rounds color 5 and 2 rounds color 6. At 22" cross, do a ½" eye in color 2, then 3 rounds color 8 and 2 rounds color 4.

At 28½" cross, do a shield eye of color 8, 4 rounds color 5, 4 rounds color 9 and 3 rounds color 6. On ends of 10" sticks, do matching ojos of ¼" color 6, 3 rounds color 1, 3 rounds color 3.

At top cross, do a ½" eye of color 1, then 3 rounds color 9 and 2 rounds color 2.
Using a strand of color 2 and color 5, extend wrap all exposed sticks.

Trim each ojo end with shooting tassels (See MAKING ENDS NEAT) using only 12 strands of different colored yarn and wrapping with color 1. Attach loop behind the top cross.

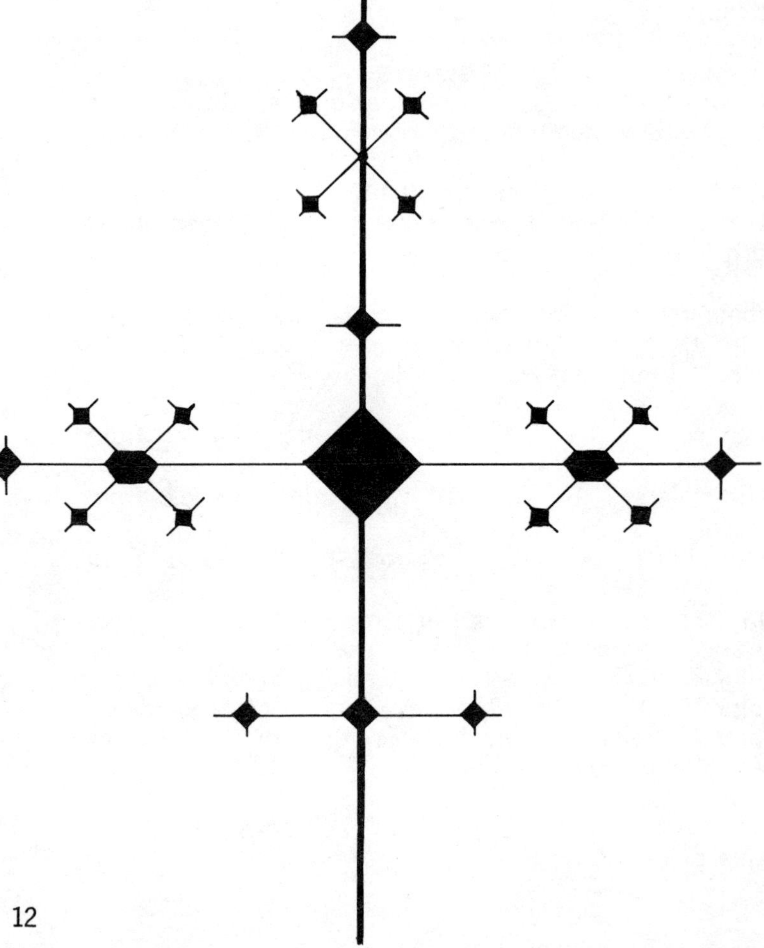

SUN GOD

STICKS:

Cut two 18" and two 24" sticks in narrow width.

NOTCHING:

Notch each stick in center.

GLUING:

Glue each pair of sticks into a basic ojo. Place larger ojo below smaller, drill small hole through center and fasten together with ¾x6-32 machine screw and nut, spacing evenly. Paint sticks black.

PROCEDURE:

Measure 2" from center on each arm and put a small amount of glue on back side. Attach color 1 on arm 1 and top wrap each arm being careful to fasten yarn to glue spots, leaving center open. Do two rounds. With color 2, starting on arm 5, top wrap for two rounds. With color 3 on arm 2, top wrap for two rounds. With color 4 on arm 6 top wrap 2 rounds. With color 5 on arm 3, top wrap 2 rounds.

Attach color 2 to arm 4 and do 6 rounds in star wrap, (See TERMINOLOGY) going under every other arm. With color 3 on arm 4, star wrap for 3 rounds. With color 4 on arm 4, star wrap 3 rounds.

Attach color 1 on arm 1 and begin Figure 8 top wrap, going under and around arm 5, over and around arm 2, taking 2 turns, over and around arm 5, under and around arm 1 with 2 turns. Repeat twice more. Glue off on arm 1. Attach color 1 on arm 3, go under and around arm 7, over and around arm 4 with 2 turns, over and around arm 7, under and around arm 3 with 2 turns. Repeat twice more. Glue off on arm 3.

Attach color 1 on arm 6 and extend wrap 1". With color 1 on arm 8 extend wrap 1".

With color 5 on arm 1, top wrap for 3 rounds. With color 2 on arm 8, top wrap 5 rounds. With color 3 on arm 1, top wrap 3 rounds. With color 4 on arm 5, top wrap for 3 rounds. With color 5 on arm 2 top wrap 4 rounds.

With color 2 on arm 1, star wrap for 8 rounds. With color 3 on arm 1, star wrap for 3 rounds. With color 4 on arm 1 star wrap for 3 rounds.

With color 1 on arm 2, figure 8 top wrap under and around arm 6, over and around arm 3 with 2 turns, over and around arm 6, under and around arm 2 with 2 turns. Repeat twice more. Glue off on arm 2. With color 1 on arm 4, figure 8 top wrap under and around arm 8, over and around arm 1 with 2 turns, over and around arm 8, under and around arm 4 with 2 turns. Repeat twice more. Glue off on arm 4.

With color 1, extend wrap arms 5 and 7 for 1½". (Check measurements from center and adjust wraps to make equal work on all arms.)

With color 5 on arm 1, top wrap each arm for 3 rounds. With color 2, top wrap for 3 rounds, with color 3 top wrap for 3 rounds, with color 4 top wrap for 4 rounds, with color 5 top wrap for 4 rounds.

Leave ends untrimmed. Fasten on a center decoration — a ceramic sun god, a beaded circle, a small shield ojo — whatever you wish! Conceal top hanger in a shooting tassel (See MAKING ENDS NEAT) on arm 3.

COLOR CHART

1. Rose
2. Cream
3. Yellow
4. Orange
5. Bright red

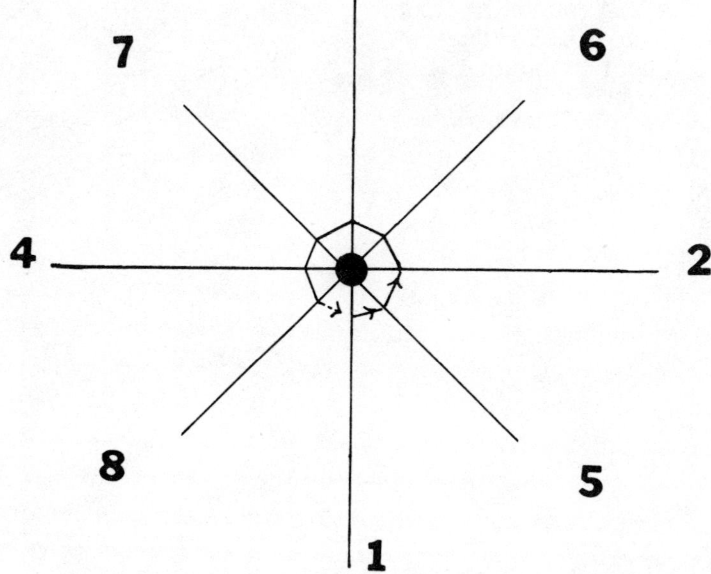

NORDISKA

This ojo is copied from a 200 year old festival ojo now in The Nordiska Museum in Stockholm, Sweden. The author was allowed to measure and photograph the intriguing mobile while on a recent trip to Scandinavia. Made of straw, the ojo is an important part of festive, Scandinavian life.

Upper Ojo

STICKS:
Cut three 14" long ¼" round dowels.

NOTCHING:
Using a rat tail file, make a shallow notch at center.

GLUING:
Using template, glue at 60⁰ angles to make a round ojo. Leave natural color but designate one end as arm 1 with a small piece of masking tape.

NOTE:
The entire Nordiska ojo is top wrapped in fine yarns such as one strand of Persian. The one pictured was made of a fine nubby acrylic from Israel, fine sport and Bucilla multi.

PROCEDURE:
With color 1, wrap a Six Point Eye (See ADVANCED TERMINOLOGY) for 1¾" (See HOW TO MEASURE).

Working all in top wrap and attaching colors on arm 1, being careful to glue on and off snugly, do the following: 3 rounds of color 2, 6 rounds of color 3, 2 rounds of color 4, 4 rounds of color 5, 5 rounds of color 6, 7 rounds of color 3, 6 rounds of color 7, 8 rounds of color 8, 5 rounds of color 9, 8 rounds of color 3, 10 rounds of color 10, 5 rounds of color 6, 6 rounds of color 2, 4 rounds of color 7, 6 rounds of color 3, 4 rounds of color 8, 3 rounds of color 4, and finish with color 5 (about 6 rounds.) Lay aside.

COLOR CHART
1. Light rust (fine silk) bouclé
2. Bright green bouclé
3. Chartreuse fine sport
4. Dark rust bouclé
5. Yellow bouclé
6. Brown bouclé
7. Orange bouclé
8. Teal bouclé
9. Red bouclé
10. Bucilla multi in yellow/orange
11. White bouclé
12. Purple bouclé

Lower Ojo

STICKS:
Cut three sticks 9" long of ⅛" round dowel. Do not notch.

GLUING:
Using template, glue at 45⁰ angle.

PROCEDURE:
With color 2, do a ¾" eye.

Working in top wrap and gluing each color on arm 1, work as follows:
3 rounds of color 9, 2 rounds of color 11, 2 rounds of color 12, 3 rounds of color 3, 4 rounds of color 7, 4 rounds of color 10, 4 rounds of color 8, 5 rounds of color 3, 4 rounds of color 2, 2 rounds of color 4, 4 rounds of color 10, 4 rounds of color 12, 5 rounds of color 3, 4 rounds of color 5, and finish with color 2 (about 3 rounds.)

A

UPPER OJO

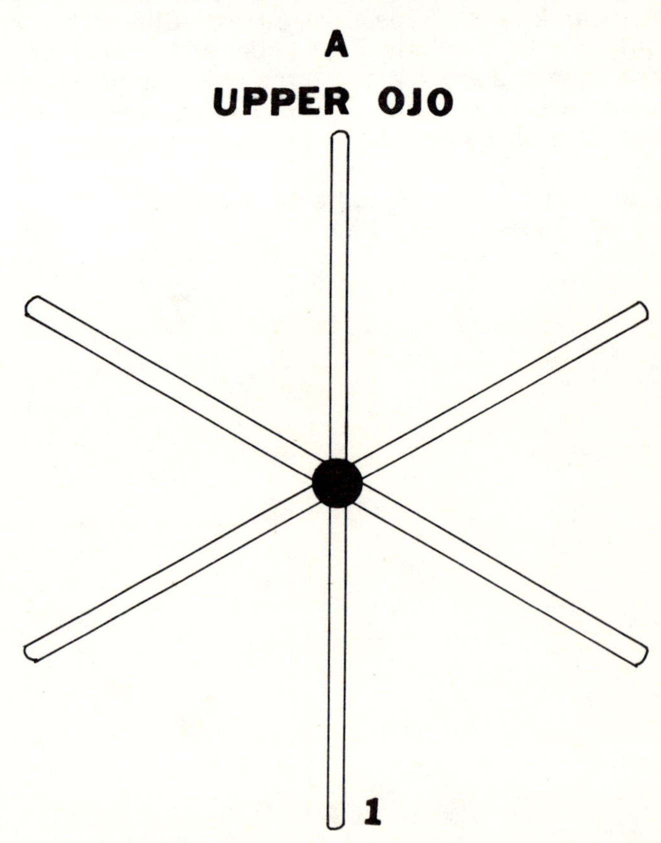

Hanging Ojos

STICKS:
Cut Twenty-six 4" sticks of ⅛" round dowel. Do not notch.

GLUING:
Glue to make 13 basic ojos. Leave natural.

PROCEDURE:
Using all Double Wrap (See ADVANCED TERMINOLOGY) make a ¾" eye in different colors on each ojo. Using a variety of colors, do two double rounds of five colors to complete each ojo.

B

LOWER OJO

1

FINISHING:
With steel crochet hook #0, using colors 1 and 5 together, make a chain 6" long leaving 3" of thread on each end.

Leaving a 1½" starting thread make thirteen 4" long chains of colors 1 and 5.

Leaving 1½" starting threads make a chain 4" long and slip stitch 2" from end (finished "noose chain" will measure 3"). Do 51 of these.

Using small plastic asters not larger than 1" in diameter, in varying colors, thread two flowers on each "noose chain". Tie one chain to each hanging ojo arms 1, 2, and 4.

Thread two flowers on each 4" chain and attach to arm 3 of each hanging ojo. Use glue to secure all attached chains.

Attach each hanging ojo to each arm of the upper and lower ojos, reserving one. Attach one "noose" chain at center of each space between arms of upper and lower ojos by tying over the last two top wraps.

Bring the three inch ends of one end of the six inch chain up through the center of the upper ojo. Tie snugly. Tie the other three inch ends through the center of the lower ojo being sure both ojos have right side downward. Tie snugly around center. Fasten 13th hanging ojo to center of bottom ojo.

Hang either by tying a nylon thread at center of upper ojo, or crochet a chain the desired length and end with hanging loop.

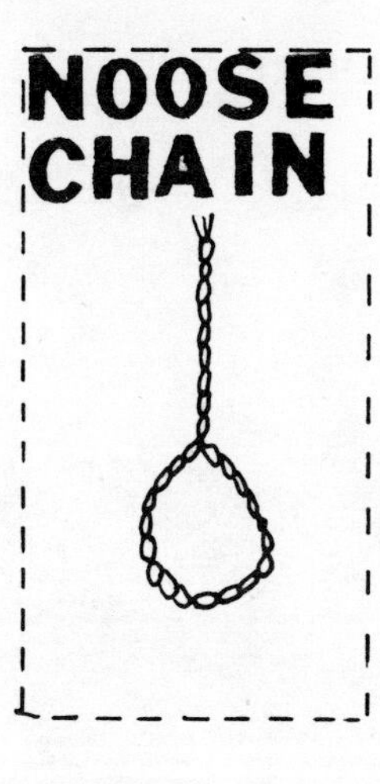

LIGHTNING SHIELD

STICKS:

Cut four 18" sticks, narrow width.

NOTCHING:

Notch each stick in center.

GLUING:

Glue together to make 2 basic ojos. Paint bright red.

PROCEDURE:

On each ojo, make a ¾" eye in color 1.

Drill a small hole partway through the uncovered centers of each ojo (the back side), break off a small piece of a wood toothpick, insert with glue in holes and place ojos together with finished eyes facing out. Check spacing carefully (See diagram) and let dry.

Attach color 2 behind arm 1. Top wrap over each arm for 4 rounds. Glue off on arm 1.

Attach color 3 behind arm 1 and top wrap each arm for 2 rounds. Glue off.

Attach color 1 behind arm 5 and wing wrap on arms 5 and 7 for ¾". Repeat wing wraps on arms 2 and 4, 6 and 8, and 3 and 1.

Attach color 2 behind arm 1 and begin star wrap. (See TERMINOLOGY) Do 5 rounds. Trim with two rounds star wrap in color 3.

Attach color 2 on arm 5 and star wrap. Do five rounds. Trim with 2 rounds of color 3 in star wrap.

Attach color 1 to arm 7 and wing wrap for 1" on arms 7 and 5. Repeat wing wraps on arms 4 and 2, 8 and 6 and 1 and 3.

Attach color 2 to arm 8 and do 5 rounds in star wrap. Trim with 2 rounds star wrap in color 3. Attach color 2 on arm 1 and do 5 rounds of star wrap. Trim with 2 rounds star wrap in color 3.

Attach color 1 behind arm 4 and wing wrap for 1" on arms 4 and 2. Repeat wing wrap on arms 8 and 6, 1 and 3 and 5 and 7.

FROM NOW ON, TAKE TWO TURNS AROUND EVERY ARM BOTH ON WING WRAP AND STAR WRAP.
Attach color 2 behind arm 8. Do 6 rounds star wrap and trim with 2 rounds of star wrap color 3. Attach color 2 on arm 1 and do 6 rounds of star wrap. Trim with 2 rounds star wrap in color 3.

Attach color 1 on arm 2 and wing wrap arms 2 and 4 for 2". Repeat wing wrap on arms 6 and 8, 3 and 1 and 7 and 5. ON LAST ROW OF EACH WING WRAP, TAKE ONLY ONE TURN.

Trim by gluing large red wooden balls (at least 1" in diameter) to each arm. They should be big enough to slide over sticks.

COLOR CHART

1. Red
2. Cream
3. Brown

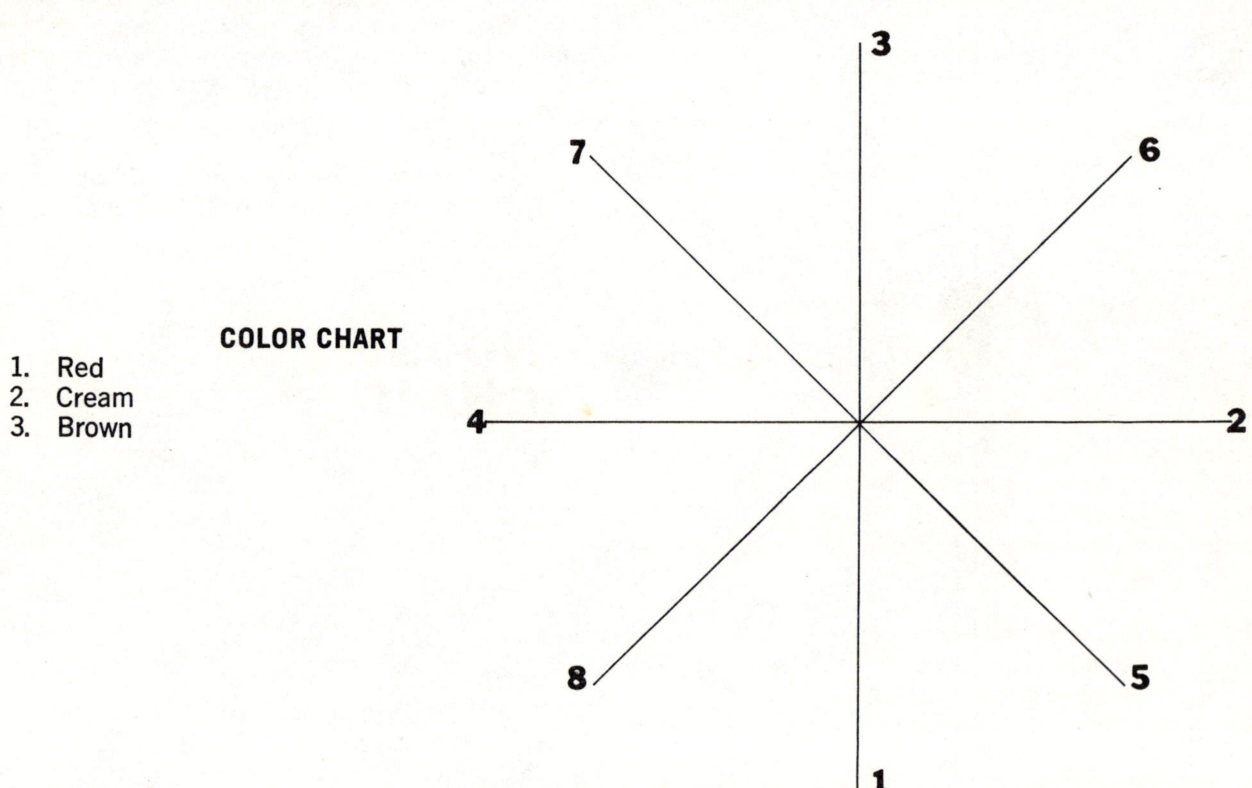

CHAIN OF COMMAND

One of the most versatile ojo designs, it is possible to use this as a vertical or horizontal hanging. The two larger ojos may be used either horizontally or vertically with the smaller center ojo in contrasting position.

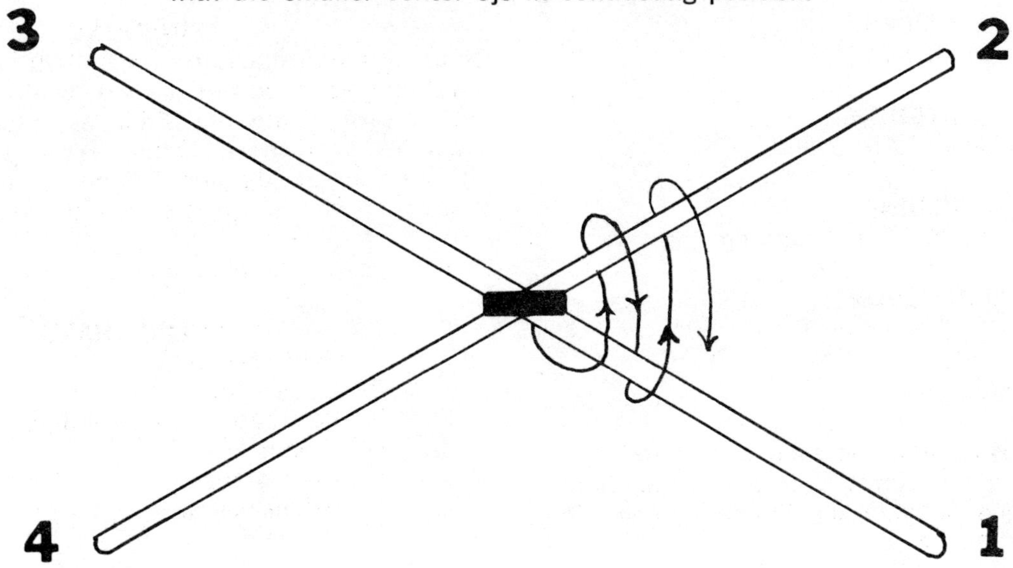

STICKS:
Cut four 16½" and two 14½" sticks in wide width.

NOTCHING:
Using template, notch each pair of sticks in center at 45° angle to the vertical. Arrow ends.

GLUING:
Glue sticks together to make 3 ojos. Paint bright red.

PROCEDURE:
For the two larger ojos, wrap an oblong eye (See TERMINOLOGY) in color 1 to measure 1⅛". Working only on arms 4 and 1 attach color 2 on arm 4 and begin figure 8 wrap. (See TERMINOLOGY) Work 1" (about 12 turns).

Attach color 3 on arm 4 and figure 8 wrap for ¾" (about 10 turns). Attach color 4 on arm 4, figure 8 wrap for 5 turns. Attach color 1 on arm 4 and figure 8 wrap for 4 turns.

Working on arms 2 and 3, attaching yarn to arm 2, wrap to match work on arms 4 and 1.

Attach color 5 to arm 4, back wrap for 7 rounds. Attach color 2 to arm 4, back wrap for 3 rounds. Do not glue off. Extend wrap arm 4 for ¾". *Without gluing off, back wrap to next arm, and extend wrap for ¾". Repeat from * twice and glue off on arm 4.

Attaching to arm 1 top wrap with color 3 for 4 rounds, with color 6 for 4 rounds, with color 2 for 4 rounds. Do not glue off. Change to back wrap and do 8 rounds. Attach color 3 on arm 1, do 2 rounds. Finish with 3 rounds of color 4.

Make a matching 16½" ojo.

For the smaller ojo, make a 1⅛" oblong eye in color 1. Working arms 4 and 1, figure 8 wrap with color 2 for 1". With color 3, figure 8 wrap for ½" (about 7 turns). With color 4, figure 8 wrap for 4 turns. With color 1, figure 8 wrap for 3 turns. Make matching wraps on arms 2 and 3. Attaching to arm 4 with color 5, back wrap 6 rounds. With color 2, back wrap 3 rounds and without gluing off extend wrap arm 4 for ½". * Without gluing off, back wrap to next arm and extend wrap ½". Repeat from * twice, and glue off on arm 4.

Attaching color 3 on arm 1, top wrap 3 rounds. With color 6, top wrap 3 rounds. With color 2, top wrap 3 rounds. Do not glue off. Change to back wrap for 7 rounds. With color 1, back wrap 2 rounds and switch to top wrap for 3 rounds. Do 1 round of color 3 and finish with 3 rounds of color 4.

FINISHING:
Obtain 2-12" and 1-10" metal macramé rings. Wind with avocado rug yarn. Glue the 2 larger ojos on the 12" circles and the smaller ojo on the 10" circle spacing carefully. Tie for additional security.

Using at least 3 gold anodized drapery chain links, attach smaller ojo circle between the 2 larger ones.

COLOR CHART
1. Copen blue
2. Variegated in jewel tones
3. Cream
4. Scarlet red
5. Purple
6. Emerald green

NIGHT OWL (OJO)

(See Cover Picture)

STICKS:
Cut two 24" wide width sticks.

NOTCHING:
Notch each stick in center. Arrow ends.

GLUING:
Glue together in a basic ojo. Paint dark orange.

PROCEDURE:
With color 1, make a 1½" eye.

With color 2, do 4 rounds.

With color 3, do 1" wing wraps on each pair of sticks. Working in top wrap, do 6 rounds of color 4, 5 rounds of color 5, and 5 rounds of color 6. Without gluing off, change to back wrap and do 8 rounds.

Working in back wrap, do 6 rounds of color 2, change to top wrap and do 5 rounds. Working all in back wrap, do ¾" color 1, ¾" color 3, 6 rounds of color 7, ½" color 4, 6 rounds of color 2, ½" color 5, 4 rounds of color 6, 5 rounds of color 1.

Without gluing off, add color 5 to color 1 and do 3 rounds of twist wrap (See TERMINOLOGY).

Continuing in back wrap, do 5 rounds of color 7. With color 4, do 2 rounds of back wrap and without gluing off, change to top wrap and do 5 rounds. Finish with 3 rounds of color 1, and 4 rounds of color 5 in top wrap.

FINISHING:
Obtain 2 metal macramé rings, 1-20" and 1-27", also, 7 links of gold anodized drapery chain. Cut 12 yards of color 5 yarn gift tie into 7" pieces. Fasten pieces around rings with larkshead knots. Hang smaller ring from chain on larger ring and drilling ⅛" hole in arm 3, ½" down from end of ojo, attach with extra chain link.

Now proceed with macramé owl instructions.

COLOR CHART
1. Light orange
2. Golden tan
3. Variegated yellow/orange
4. Cream
5. Dark orange
6. Bright yellow
7. Brown

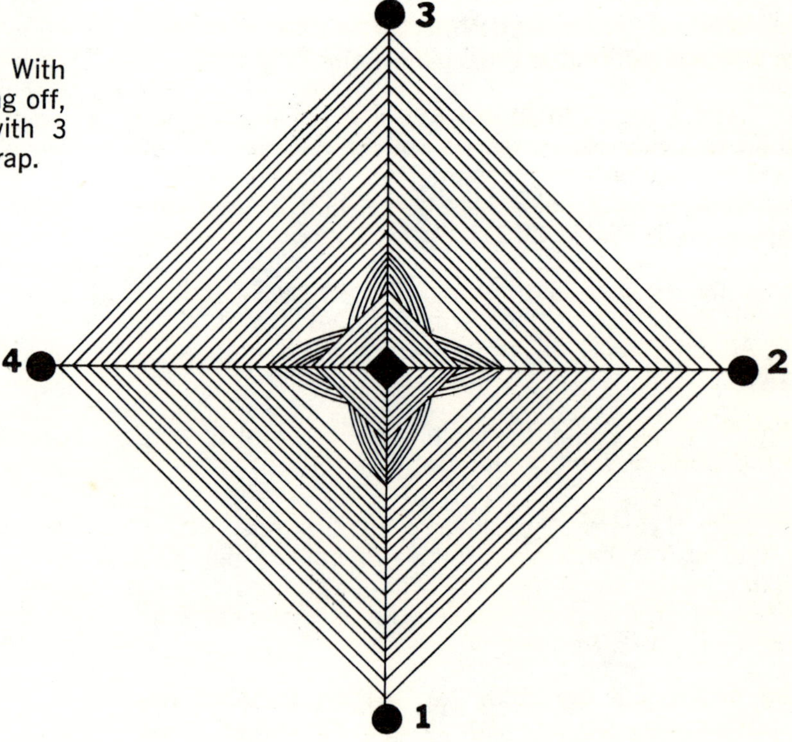

NIGHT OWL (MACRAMÉ)

OWL

Use cream colored Calcutta cord.

Cut 8 cords 4 feet long for center.
Cut 8 cords 5 feet long for outsides.

Larkshead on a twig with 4 of the longer cords on right, 4 on left.

Do two rows of alternate square knots across head.

Working with four outside cords, right and left, make 8 square knots. On center 4 cords, make 10 square knots.

Dropping two outside cords, square knot across to join.

Using two outside cords, square knot across.

Now using four outside cords on each side, square knot 17 times. Using next 4 cords on each side, do 16 square knots.

On center cords, do alternate square knots until you have 5 complete edgings (10 rows of knots)

Now join by dropping two outside cords on each side and square knotting across, then on next row pick up outside cords and square knot across.

Using cords 8 and 9 in from each side, do double half hitch on tree branch.

Divide cords so center ones cross and tie overhand knot under each foot.

Using the fluff of guinea hen feathers, cover breast of owl by inserting quill under knot and securing with small amount of glue.

Using the full guinea hen feather, insert one feather in each larkshead knot on top of head and secure with glue.

Make eyes by wrapping a 1" diameter ring with cord, then gluing the tips of guinea hen feathers around eyes.

Finish with medium wooden bead and glue in place on face.

Fasten owl to ojo by gluing top branch to inner ring and reinforcing with fine florist wire concealed under head feathers.

LARKSHEAD

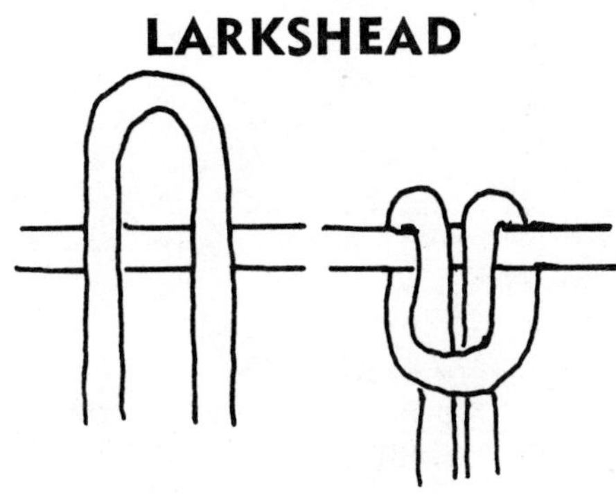

SQUARE KNOT

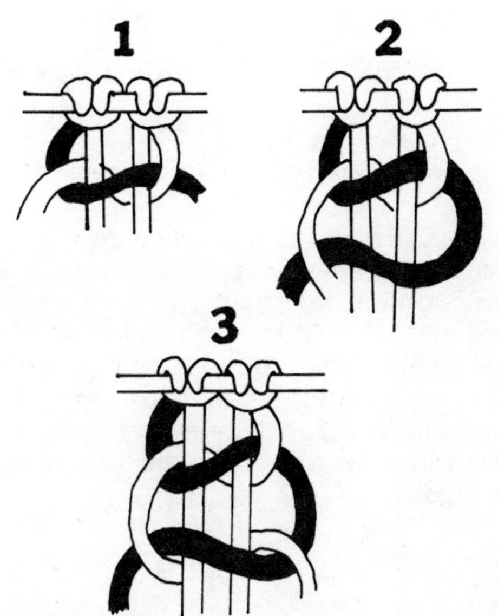

ALTERNATING SQUARE KNOTS

THE THREE MASTER

STICKS:
Cut one 24", one 18", one 12" and one 4" stick in narrow width.

NOTCHING:
Notch the 4", 12" and 18" sticks in the center. Notch the 24" stick 6" down, in the center and turning stick half turn, 6" up.

GLUING:
Glue 18" stick at top notch, 4" stick at center notch and the 12" stick at the right angle notch. Paint sticks deep blue.

PROCEDURE:
Make a 1" double eye (See TERMINOLOGY) in color 1 at each cross.

With color 2, outline with two rounds on each eye, both sides.

With color 2, wrap exposed stick between each cross.

With color 3 on arm 1, go over and around arm 2, over and around arm 6, follow eye around arm 3, follow eye around arm 5, over and around arm 4, follow eye around arm 1, (Diagram A). Half turn ojo to left so back side is facing you. Follow eye around arm 4, up and over arm 5, follow eye around arm 3, follow eye around arm 6, over and around arm 2, follow eye around arm 1. (Diagram B). Half turn ojo to left so right side is again facing you. Do 2 rounds.

Following the winding pattern, do 3 rounds of color 4, 2 rounds of color 5, 2 rounds of color 6, 2 rounds of color 2, 3 rounds of color 1, 2 rounds of color 6. (BE SURE TO COMPLETE DIAGRAM B EACH TIME)

Begin space wrap by taking an extra turn around arms 5 and 6 each time. Do 3 rounds of color 4, 2 rounds of color 2, 2 rounds of color 1.

Taking only one turn around each arm, do 3 rounds of color 5.

FINISHING:
Insert a small screw eye in top of arm 3 and attach a small fishing swivel, using a small jump ring.

COLOR CHART
1. Blue tweed
2. Bright rose
3. Cream
4. Soft blue
5. Moss green
6. Sunny yellow

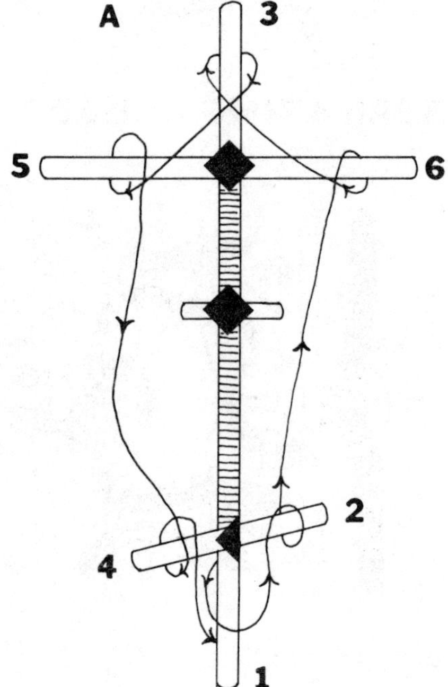

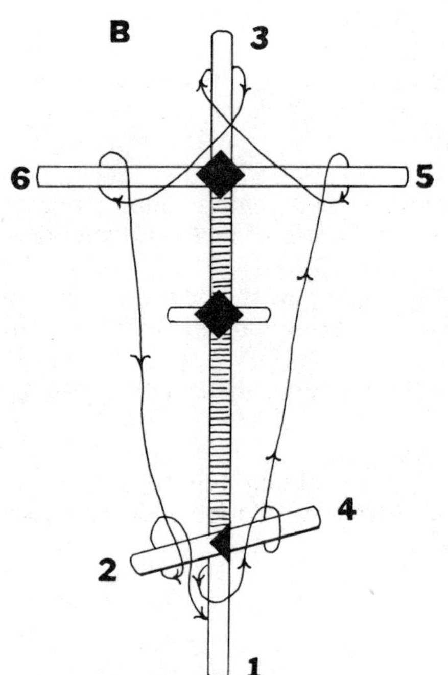

SPINNING TOP

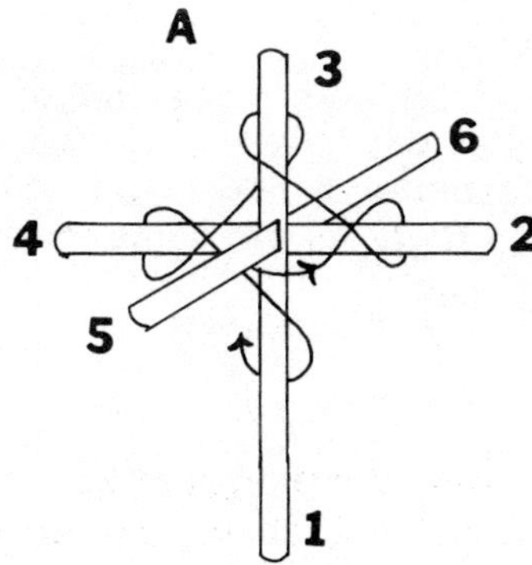

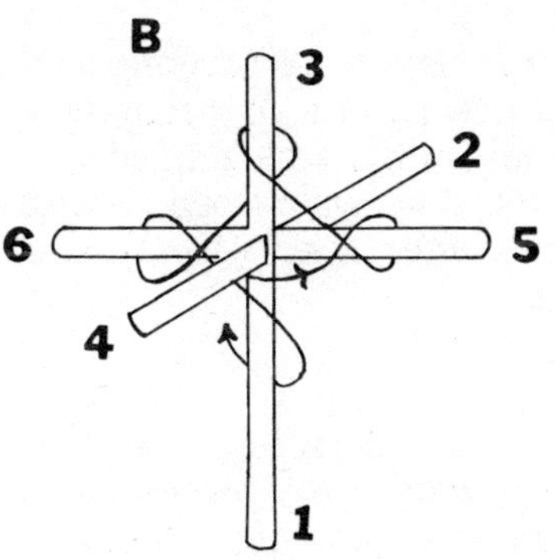

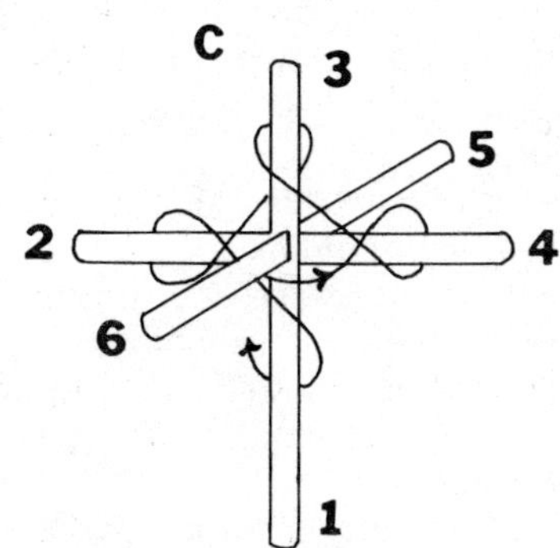

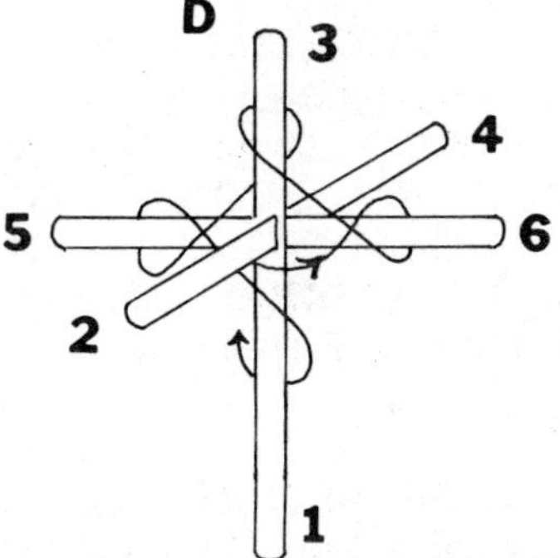

STICKS:
Cut one 24", one 16" and two 8" sticks in narrow width.

NOTCHING:
Notch the 24" stick 8" down from top and 16" stick in center.

GLUING:
Glue the two notched sticks together to form a kite shape. Cut the head from a 2" nail and file to point. Drill a small hole through the center of the glued notches and into one end of each of the 8" sticks. Fill each hole with glue, insert nail through notch hole and into each 8" stick to make a right angle cross with kite shape. Check carefully to see each stick is square with the adjoining stick. Let dry overnight. Paint bright blue.

METHOD:
Following **Diagram A,** attach yarn back of arm 1, wind over arm 2, arm 3 and arm 4, ending by twirling around arm 1. Give the ojo a quarter turn to the right, disregard the right angle sticks and follow **Diagram B,** wrapping over arm 5, arm 3, arm 6 and twirling around arm 1. Rotate the ojo a quarter turn to the right. Follow **Diagram C** wrapping over arm 4, arm 3, arm 2 and twirling around arm 1. Give ojo a quarter turn to the right and follow **Diagram D,** wrapping arm 6, arm 3, arm 5 and twirling around arm 1. This completes one round. (Hint: Clip a small clothespin to the right arm each time you start a new quarter turn. This helps you keep track of which Diagram you are on.)

Note: If you think of this ojo as a simple kite ojo, ignoring the right angle sticks as you wind, it will be easy to do.

PROCEDURE:
With color 1, wrap an eye of 5 rounds.

Attach color 2 behind arm 1 (always glue off and glue new color on behind arm 1) and start Kite Wrap with two turns on arm 1 and one turn on all other arms. Do 4 complete rounds.

Attach color 3 and do 2 complete rounds.
Attach color 1 and do 2 complete rounds.
Attach color 4 and do 4 complete rounds.
Attach color 2 and do 2 complete rounds.
Attach color 1 and do 4 complete rounds.
Attach color 3 and do 3 complete rounds.

From now to end, increase one round on all but arm 3 taking one turn on arm 3, three turns on arm 1 and two turns on arms 2, 4, 5 and 6.

Attach color 4 and do 4 complete rounds.

Attach color 2 and finish ojo with 2 complete rounds.

Trim with 1½" red and white plastic fishing floats on arms 2, 4, 5, 6.

Attach small swivel, obtainable in sporting goods and hobby stores, at top by inserting a small screw eye in arm 3 and using a jump ring.

COLOR CHART
1. Bucilla Frisky in pink/red/white combination
2. Royal blue
3. White
4. Bright red

ZAKOPANE

This ojo comes from the Tatra Mountain region of Poland and is used at festival time to decorate the household. They are made not by the women, but by the shepherds while in the fields. The wool used throughout is a fine tapestry yarn, but other specialty yarns in thin weights may be substituted.

The original framework was made not of wood, but of two weights of wire coat hangers. If wire is used, notch with a file and fasten with household cement, allowing to dry 24 hours. Then follow same directions as for wood.

STICKS:

Using ¼" round dowels, cut 3 pieces 13" long. Using ⅛" round dowels, cut 14 pieces 4½" long.

NOTCHING:

With a rattail file, very lightly notch all 4½" sticks in center. Using Template, notch 13" sticks in center to fit 60° angles (making an evenly spaced circle).

GLUING:

Glue 4½" sticks to make 7 small basic ojos. Glue 13" sticks to make shield ojo.

PROCEDURE:

Using top wrap throughout on ALL ojos, make up as follows:

LARGE OJO: With color 1, wrap a 1" eye. Continuing with top wrap, make ¾" bands of color 2, color 3, color 4, color 5, color 6, and finish to end with color 8.

Small ojo A — With color 4, do 1" eye. Continuing in top wrap, make ¼" bands of color 9, color 10 and finish to end with color 11.

Small ojo B — Make a 1" eye in color 11, then ¼" bands of colors 6, 3 and finish with 2.

Small ojo C — Eye of color 10. Bands of 9, 2 and finish with 1.

Small ojo D — Eye of 4. Bands of 9, 10 and finish with 11.

Small ojo E — Eye of 11. Bands of 6, 3 and finish with 2.

Small ojo F — Eye of 10. Bands of 5, 2. Finish with 1.

Small ojo G — Eye of 8. Bands of 2, 5. Finish with 6.

ASSEMBLY #1: With a #0 crochet hook (steel) and using yarn double, crochet 3 chains 24" long of colors, 1, 2 and 9. Fold in center and wrap tightly with a strand of wool 1½ inches down to make a hanging loop. Laying large ojo upside down on table, attach each chain to two opposing arms, using the ends to tie a double square knot.

Crochet two 13" chains each of the following colors: color 3, color 2, color 8, color 4, color 6, color 9, color 7. Using a 3" pompon maker, make flat pompons (See MAKING ENDS NEAT), one each in colors 2, 3, 4, 6, 9, 11. Using 2" pompon maker, make flat pompons, 2 each of colors 2 and 4, and 4 each of colors 1, 6, 7, 8, 11. DO NOT MAKE TOO FULL.

ASSEMBLY #2: Carefully thread two different color chains over the large ojo ends four strands from the outside round. Wrap with a strand of wool ½" below the large ojo arm. Slip ends of small ojo, 3" from wrapping into chain. Check to be sure ojo is level and touch all four ends with a dab of glue to hold. BE SURE TO ATTACH SMALL OJOS SO THEY, LIKE THE UPPER LARGE ONE, HAVE RIGHT SIDE TOWARD FLOOR.

Attach a matching 2" French tassel to ends of chains.

DO NOT MAKE TOO FULL. Attach large flat pompons on top of 6 arms of large ojo. Using contrasting colors to the chains, attach matching pairs of small flat pompons on top of arms of small ojos. Hang the 7th ojo in center, using same method of assembly and same trim.

COLOR CHART

1. Pink	7. Royal blue
2. Peacock blue	8. Chartreuse
3. Soft yellow	9. White
4. Purple	10. Red
5. Cream	11. Aqua
6. Dark orange	

LARGE OJO

SMALL OJOS

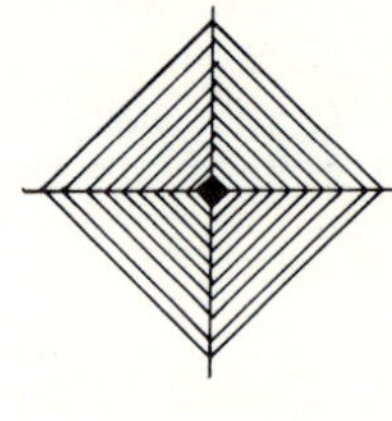

SPECTRUM

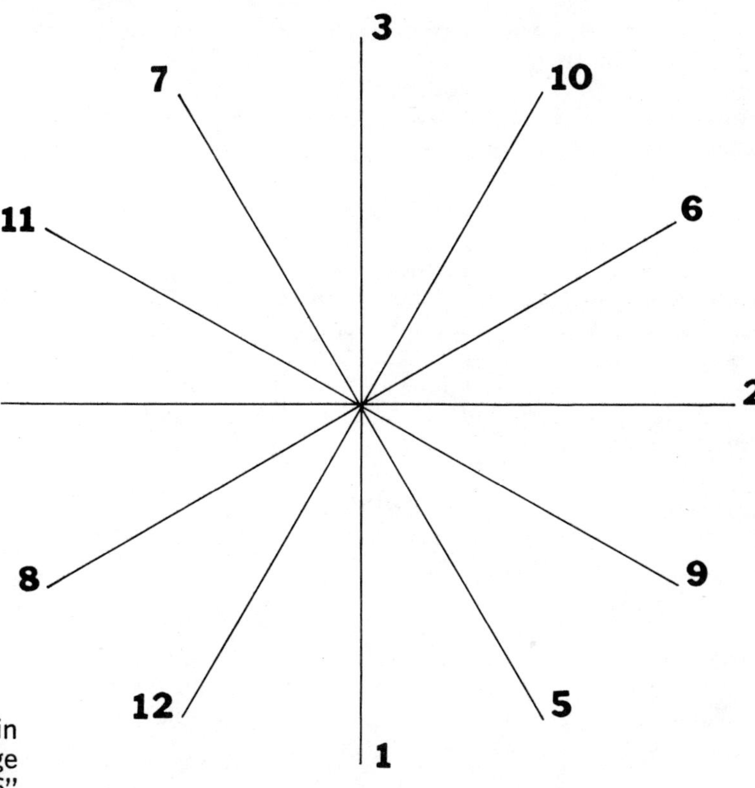

COLOR CHART
1. Bright rose
2. Two-ply variegated in rainbow shades. (The use of this weight makes dimension on this ojo)
3. Bright lavendar
4. Lime green
5. Golden yellow
6. Light blue

STICKS:
Cut six 18" sticks narrow width.

NOTCHING:
Notch all sticks in center.

GLUING:
Glue into 3 basic ojos. When dry, drill a 3/16" hole in center of each ojo. Laying ojos on template, arrange evenly at 30°, 60° and 90° angles. Fasten with a 3/16" brass screw and nut. Paint sticks light blue.

PROCEDURE:
WORKING ONLY ON THE FRONT OJO (arms 1, 2, 3 and 4), do a 1¼" eye in color 1. Adjust threads to cover screw head.

Attach color 2 on arm 5. WORKING ONLY ON BACK OJOS (omit arms 1, 2, 3, 4), backwrap each arm in rotation 1¼" from center of screw measured on back side.

Attach color 3 on arm 1 in usual manner. Attach color 4 directly below with cut end to right. Turn ojo to right side. Begin Spectrum Wrap. (See ADVANCED TERMINOLOGY) Do 3 rounds of each color and glue off on arm 1.

Attach color 5 to arm 1 in usual manner. Attach color 6 directly below with cut end to right. Turn ojo to right side. Continue in Spectrum Wrap for 3 rounds of each color.

Attach color 1 on arm 9. Top wrapping every arm, do 3 rounds.

Attach color 2 on arm 11. Star Wrap (See TERMINOLOGY) for 8 rounds.
Attach color 2 on arm 4. Star Wrap for 8 rounds.
Attach color 2 on arm 8. Star Wrap for 8 rounds.

Attach color 4 on arm 1 in usual manner. Attach color 3 directly below with cut end to right. Turn ojo to right side. Spectrum Wrap for 3 rounds of each color.

Attach color 6 on arm 1 in the usual manner. Attach color 5 directly below with cut end to right. Turn ojo to right side. Spectrum Wrap for 3 rounds of each color.

Attach color 1 on arm 12. With top wrap on every arm, do 4 rounds.

Attach color 2 on arm 11. Triple Star Wrap (See ADVANCED TERMINOLOGY) for ¾". Attach color 2 on arm 4. Triple Star Wrap for ¾". Attach color 2 on arm 8. Triple Star Wrap for ¾".

Attach color 3 on arm 1 in the usual manner. Attach color 4 directly below with cut end to right. Spectrum Wrap for 3 rounds of each color.
Attach color 5 on arm 1 in usual manner. Attach color 6 directly below with cut end to right. Spectrum Wrap for 3 rounds each color.

Attach color 1 on arm 12. Top wrap every arm for 5 rounds.

Attach color 2 on arm 11. Triple Star Wrap for ½". Attach color 2 on arm 4. Triple Star Wrap for ½". Attach color 2 on arm 8. Triple Star Wrap for ½".

Finish by gluing small plastic asters in rainbow colors on each arm.

Popsicle Ojos

STICKS:

Twenty nine popsicle sticks (available in most craft shops), 4½" long.

Wound Ojos

GLUING:

Glue two sticks together at center to make a basic ojo #1. Glue two together with cross stick 1¾" down center stick to make kite ojo #2. Glue two sticks together at center at 45⁰ angle of template to make an X for ojo #3. Glue three sticks together at center on 60⁰ angle of template to make a shield ojo #4.

PROCEDURE:

(Ojos #1, 2 and 4 are double wrapped throughout. See ADVANCED TERMINOLOGY).

Ojo #1. Paint sticks yellow. With color 1 wind a ½" double eye (See TERMINOLOGY). With color 2, double wrap for ¼". With color 3, extend wrap all arms for ⅜". With color 4, finish with 3 rounds of space double wrap, taking 2 turns on arms 2 and 4 each time.

Ojo #2. Paint sticks green. With color 3, make a ½" double eye. Space double wrap taking 2 turns around arm 1, with color 5 until 1" out on arm 2 from center. With color 2, do 4 rounds. Finish with 2 rounds of color 8.

Ojo #3. Paint sticks blue. With color 5, double wrap an oblong eye for ½". Making both sides match (arms 4 and 1, and 3 and 2), figure eight wrap (See TERMINOLOGY) for ⅜" in color 1. With color 6, continue figure eight wrap for ⅜", with color 7 for ¼" and finish with 3 rounds of color 8.

Ojo #4. Paint sticks white. With color 2, do a ⅜" double eye. Wrapping every arm in succession, do ⅜" of color 8. With color 10 do 3 rounds and finish with 4 rounds of color 6.

Animal Ojos

GLUING:

Mark sixteen popsicle sticks 1" in from each end. Glue into square frame at marks. When thoroughly dry, turn ojos ¼ turn, mark two lower sticks 2" in and put glue on marks. Mark four sticks 1½" in from each end and place across square frame to form base for animals.

Paint each ojo to match one of the wound ojos.

FINISHING:

Drill a small hole in the top of wound ojos arm 3 on ojos 1, 2 and 4. Drill a hole in ojo 3, arms 3 and 2. Drill a hole in each animal ojo where two sticks cross at top.

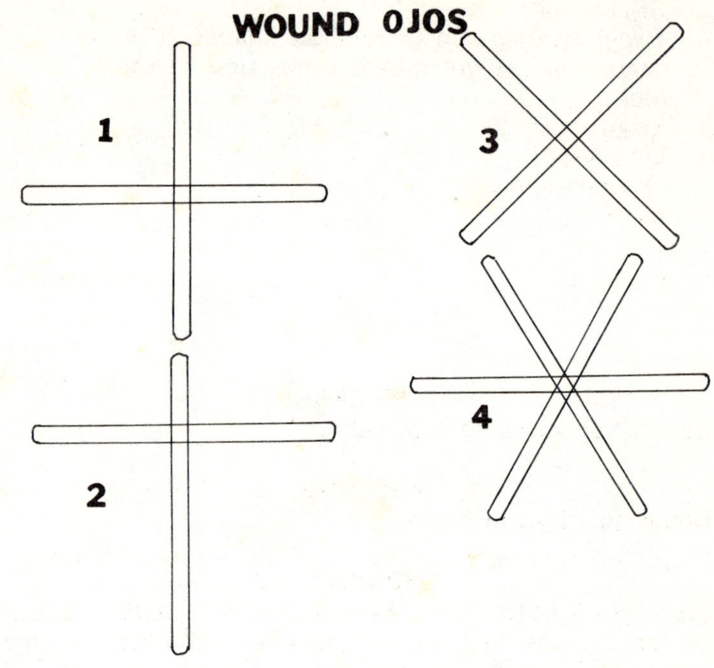

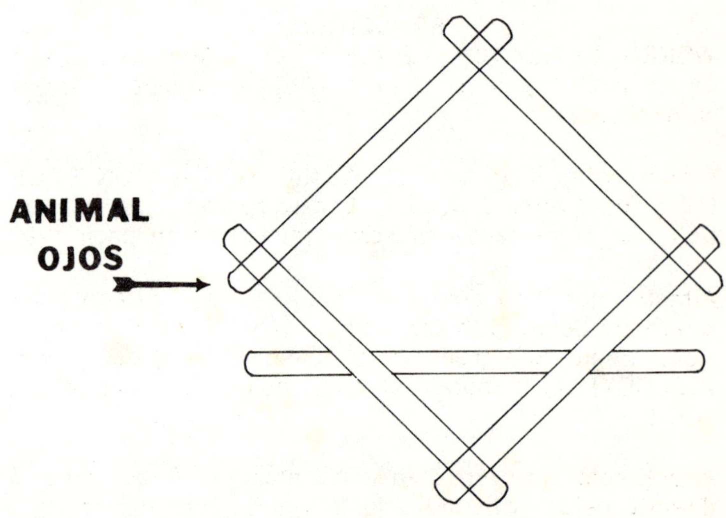

COLOR CHART

1. Orange fine silk boucle'
2. Lime green fine silk boucle'
3. Peacock blue fine silk boucle'
4. Reddish brown boucle'
5. Bucilla multi yellow/white/orange
6. Light green sport
7. Purple fine silk boucle'
8. Yellow fine silk boucle'
9. Rust fine silk boucle'
10. Tangerine fine silk boucle'

Center Ojo

STICKS:
Cut one 12", one 6" and two 4" sticks in narrow width.

NOTCHING:
Notch 12" stick three inches in from each end. Turning a quarter turn, notch on side at center point. Notch three smaller sticks in center. Paint sticks yellow.

GLUING:
Glue two 4" sticks at upper and lower notch of 12" stick. Glue 6" stick at side notch so it is at right angles to other sticks.

PROCEDURE:
With color 1, double wrap a ½" eye at each cross point. With same color extend wrap exposed stick between eyes.

METHOD:
Glue color 2 behind arm 1 and bring to front. Holding firmly by arm 8, go over and around arm 2, cross the center stick and go over and around arm 7. Recross the center stick and go over and around arm 3, over and around arm 4, over and around arm 5, over and around arm 7, over and around arm 6, over and around arm 1 with a half turn.

Now holding ojo by arm 7, repeat the pattern by going over and around arm 6, cross the center stick, going over and around arm 8, recross the center stick going over and around arm 5, over and around arm 4, over and around arm 3, over and around arm 8, over and around arm 2, over and around arm 1 with a half turn.

Holding by arm 8, repeat the diagrams A and B for a complete pattern.

Continue wrapping in this fashion, changing colors on arm 1 as desired. **BE SURE YOU HAVE COMPLETED DIAGRAM B BEFORE CHANGING COLOR.**

Color rotation should be three rounds of color 3, three rounds of color 1, two rounds of color 5, two rounds of color 10, two rounds of color 7, two rounds of color 2, two rounds of color 9, and finish with two rounds of color 10.

FINISHING:
Drill a small hole in arm 8. Insert a 40" piece of color 8, knot with square knot at end of stick.
Cut five pieces of color 8 for mini wound ojos 11" long. Pull one piece through each drilled hole. Cut four pieces of color 8 for animal ojos 12" long and thread through drilled holes.

ASSEMBLY:
Obtain a 10" macramé ring. Using three packages of yellow Yarn Gift Tie, cut 7" pieces saving one yard. Cut this into three 12" pieces. With Larkshead knot (See TERMINOLOGY), fasten 7" pieces onto ring, saving one piece. When ring is covered lay on template and attach a 12" piece at the 120° points. Tie securely. Gather the three pieces and tie with simple finger knot. Using the extra 7" piece, separate one strand and use to tie the other two strands to the triple hanger, forming a hanging loop.

Keeping the ring on the template, alternate the wound and the animal ojos and tie at each 45° point being sure animal ojos are all facing the same direction. In tying wound ojo #3, first tie the two strands together 2 inches above stick and clip off the two excess strings.

With a crochet hook pull string of center ojo up through hanging knot, separate ends and tie securely in place. The center ojo should hang freely below the mini ojos.

Glue an animal on the cross bar of each animal ojo. Glue Old McDonald on lower arm of center ojo and an animal on the top of right and left arms. Pull ring fringe to hang vertically. (Your variety store has sets of farm animals).

NOTCHING

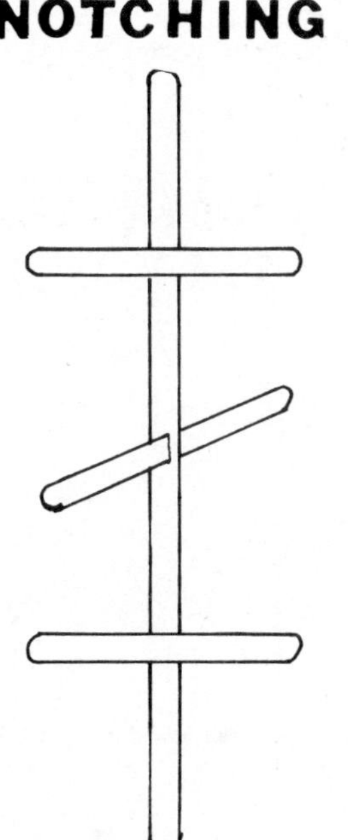

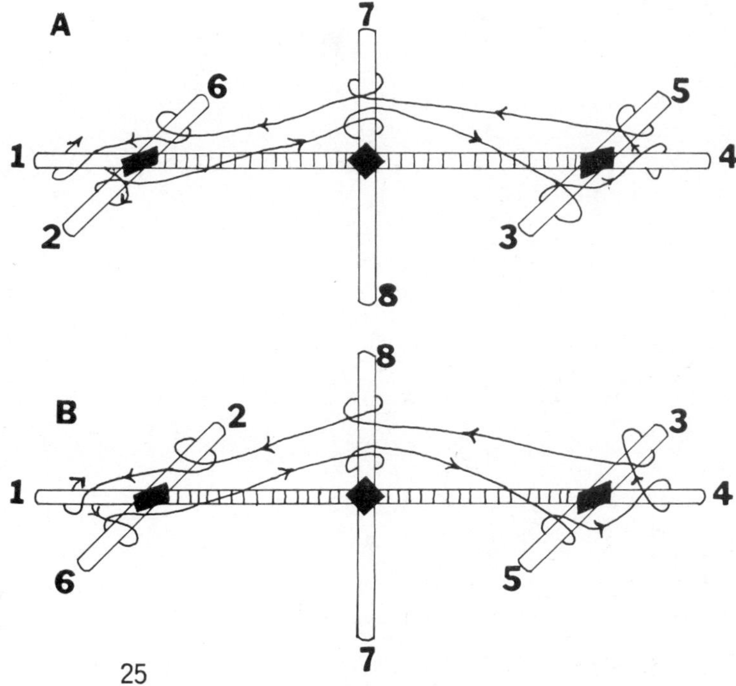

OLD McDONALD'S CAROUSEL

SPINNING TOP

ROMAN CANDLE

TOLUCA

WALL HANGING

THREE MASTER

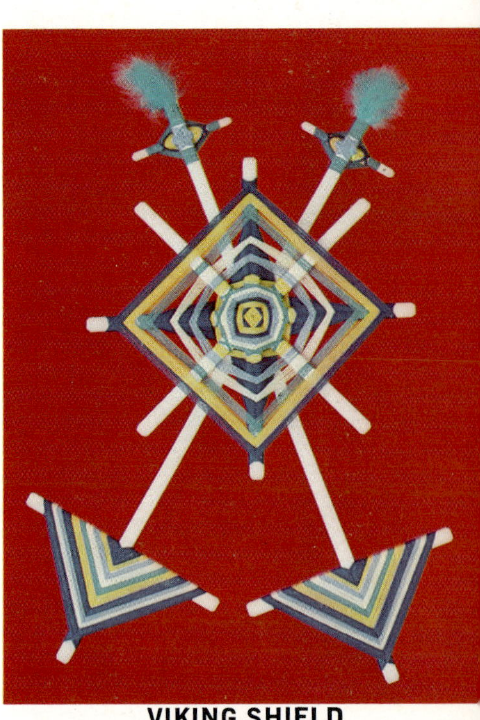

VIKING SHIELD

MIDSUMMER POLE

OPEN HOUSE

CHAIN OF COMMAND

GRANDMA'S SHOWCASE

ROOM DIVIDER

MEDICINE MAN

KUOPIO

GRANDMA'S SHOWCASE

Because the pictures are pinned on, the ojo may grow as the family grows. It can be made in colors other than nursery shades to fit in any room. It would be a delightful gift for the new mother.

STICKS:

Cut one 30" and two 18" sticks in wide width.

NOTCHING:

Notch 30" stick 8½" from each end and the 18" sticks in center.

GLUING:

Glue the 18" sticks at notches of the 30" stick. Bevel ends. Paint light rose.

PROCEDURE:

Working upper and lower crosses exactly the same, with color 1, do a ¾" eye. In top wrapping, do 4 rounds of color 2, 4 rounds of color 3 and 6 rounds of color 4.

Attach color 3 on arm 1 and do 5 rounds. Attach color 3 on arm 4 and do 5 rounds. Attach color 5 on arm 2 and do 4 rounds. Attach color 5 on arm 3 and do 4 rounds.

Attach color 6 on arm 2 and do 3 rounds. Attach color 6 on arm 5 and do 3 rounds. Attach color 2 on arm 1 and do 3 rounds. Attach color 2 on arm 4 and do 3 rounds.

Attach color 1 between the ojos and extend wrap exposed stick.

Attach color 7 to arm 1, top wrap every arm for 10 rounds. Balance of ojo is all top wrap.

Attach color 4 on arm 4, do 3 rounds. Attach color 7 on arm 4, do 8 rounds. Attach color 4 on arm 1, do 5 rounds. Attach color 7 on arm 4, do 9 rounds. Attach color 4 on arm 1, do 3 rounds. Attach color 7 on arm 4, do 8 rounds.

FINISHING:

Picture frames are antique finish brooch frames available in different sizes in craft shops. Children's pictures should be cut to fit and backed with light cardboard, before slipping into frame. Hold with a dab of glue.

Hang with a simple loop behind arm 3.

COLOR CHART

1. Pink silk straw
2. Rose silk straw
3. Pink
4. Red sparkle
5. Medium pink
6. Medium rose
7. Variegated pinks in Dazzle Aire or similar mohair type yarn.

HOLIDAY CENTERPIECE

Tree #1

STICKS:
Cut one 12" and one 18" stick, narrow width.

NOTCHING:
Notch 12" stick in center, 18" stick 6" up from bottom.

GLUING:
Glue 12" stick at notch. Paint sticks dark green.

PROCEDURE:
Using Double Tree Wrap throughout (See ADVANCED TERMINOLOGY), do 1½" half-eye in color 1. Do 3 rounds of color 2, 4 rounds of color 3, 5 rounds of color 4, 5 rounds of color 5.

Begin space tree wrap, adding one extra wind on arm 3, with color 6 for 6 rounds, 3 rounds of color 2, 4 rounds of color 5, 6 rounds of color 1, 4 rounds of color 4. Using 3 winds on arm 3, do 7 rounds of color 8 and end with 5 rounds of color 3.

Tree #2

STICKS:
Cut one 7" and one 12" stick, narrow width.

NOTCHING:
Notch 12" stick 4" up, and 7" stick in center. Glue and paint as for tree #1.

PROCEDURE:
Using Double Tree Wrap throughout, do a ¾" half-eye in color 7. With color 8, do 7 rounds. Beginning space wrap, adding one extra wrap on arm 3, do 4 rounds of color 6, 2 rounds of color 2. Adding one more wrap on arm 3 (taking 3 turns around each time) do 2 rounds of color 9, 3 rounds of color 5, 4 rounds of color 8.

COLOR CHART
1. Green bouclé
2. Fine gold metallic
3. Fine green tweed
4. Moss green
5. Light green sport weight
6. Nile green
7. Silk blend green and white
8. Candy stripe silk blend red and white
9. Green mohair blend with brown tones
10. Bright red

Tree #3

STICKS:
Cut one 5" and one 9½" stick narrow width.

NOTCHING:
Notch 5" stick in center and 9½" stick at 4" up. Glue and paint as for tree #1.

PROCEDURE:
Using Double Tree Wrap throughout, do a ¾" half-eye with color 5. With color 2, do 3 rounds and 3 rounds of color 10. Begin space wrap adding one extra turn on arm 3 with color 8 for 2 rounds, color 1 for 3 rounds. Do 3 rounds of color 4, 2 rounds of color 2 and end with 4 rounds of color 5.

FINISHING:
Using a 9x12x2 piece of green styrofoam for base, arrange trees in staggered placement. Cover styrofoam with holly greens either real or plastic.

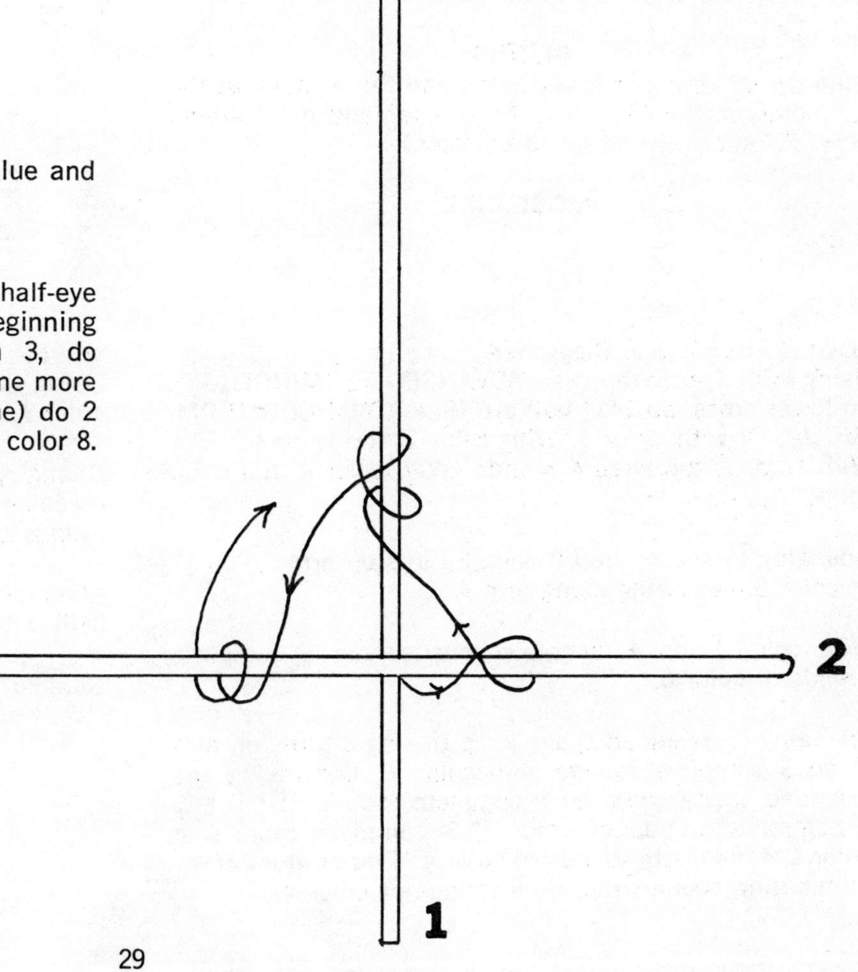

MIDSUMMER POLE

This Ojo is a version of the evergreen-wound pole used in midsummer eve celebrations in the Scandinavian countries. It may be decorated with flowers or left untrimmed.

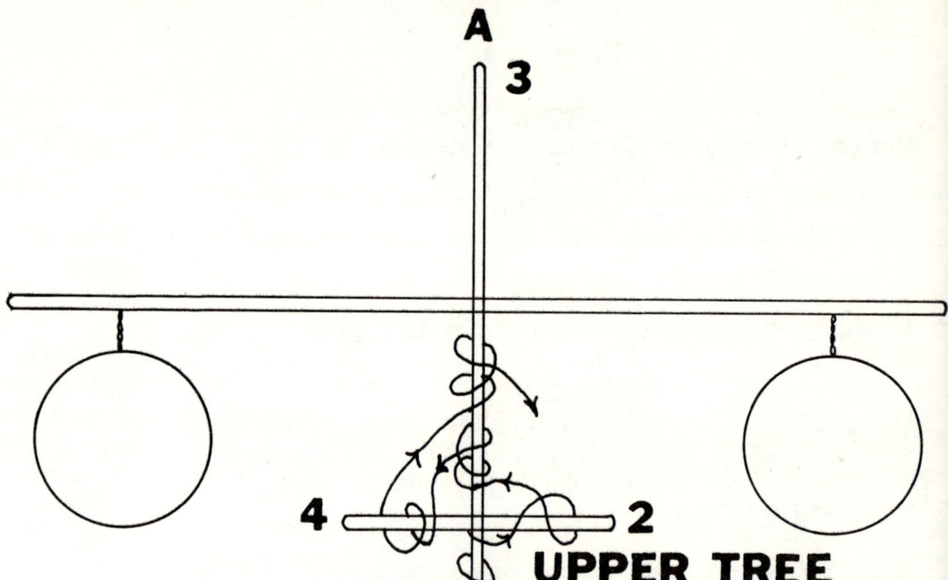

STICKS:

Cut one 9", one 18", one 36", and one 48" stick in wide width.

NOTCHING:

Notch the 48" stick at 13½", 32" and 39" up from bottom. Notch the other 3 sticks in center.

GLUING:

Glue the 18" stick at lower notch and the 9" stick at the 32" notch on the 48" stick. Arrow ends and paint green. (The 36" stick will be glued on later.)

PROCEDURE:

LOWER TREE: (See Diagram A)
Using Wall Tree Wrap (See ADVANCED TERMINOLOGY), on lower cross, do 1¾" half-eye (See ADVANCED TERMINOLOGY), with color 1. With color 2, top wrap for ½". With color 3, top wrap 4 rounds. With color 4, top wrap for ½".

Changing to space wrap (taking 2 turns on arm 3), do 1" in color 5 measuring along arm 2.

With color 1, do 4 complete rounds, and 5 complete rounds of color 6.

Changing to **extended** space wrap (taking 3 turns on arm 3), do 5 complete rounds with color 7. Continuing the extended space wrap, do 8 complete rounds of color 3, 5 complete rounds of color 2, 3 complete rounds of color 1, 4 complete rounds of color 4. Do not glue off. Eliminating space wrap, do 4 rounds of color 4.

UPPER TREE: (See Diagram A)
Using wall tree wrap, do a 1¼" half-eye in color 7. With color 4, do 4 rounds, with color 1 do 2 rounds.

Changing to space wrap, do 5 rounds of color 2, 4 rounds of color 3, 2 rounds of color 1, 4 rounds of color 4, 4 rounds of color 5.

Eliminating space wrap, finish with 5 rounds of color 6. Drill a ⅛" hole 7" in from each end on the 36" stick.

Glue 36" stick at upper notch on 48" stick.

(Ring Ojos)

STICKS:

Cut two 8" and four 5½" sticks in narrow width.

NOTCHING:

Notch the 8" sticks at 3" and 5½" up, and the 5½" sticks in center. Bevel the ends.

GLUING:

Glue the 5½" sticks at notches on 8" stick. Paint sticks green.

PROCEDURE:

(Do both ojos to match). At lower cross, make a ½" eye in color 8. At upper cross make a ½" eye in color 9.

Holding ojo by arm 1, attach color 2 on arm 2 and wall tree wrap for 4 turns. With color 1, do 2 rounds. With color 5 do 3 rounds. With color 4 do 5 rounds (or until it joins upper eye.)

Now holding ojo by arm 4, glue color 6 on arm 5. Using a half wing wrap, going behind arm 6, around arm 1, behind arm 2 and around arm 3, with two wraps around arm 3, back behind arm 2, around arm 1, behind arm 6, and around arm 5 with two wraps, do 3 rounds. With color 1, do 2 rounds. Finish with 4 rounds of color 2. (Always glue new color on arm 5 and off on arm 3.)

Drill a ⅛" hole in arm 4 and attach a link of drapery chain.

FINISHING:

Obtain two 10" metal macrame rings at a hobby or craft store. Wind tightly with color 1. Glue off. If desired, arrange a spray of plastic flowers around top half of ring, tying in place with matching yarn.

Using 2 links of drapery chain in holes on 36" stick, attach rings to cross arm. Using 3 more links for each ring, insert covered ring in center link and attach the small ojos in the center of the rings. If desired, trim lower 3 arms with small flowers.

Fasten a saw-tooth picture hanger to back of main cross arms.

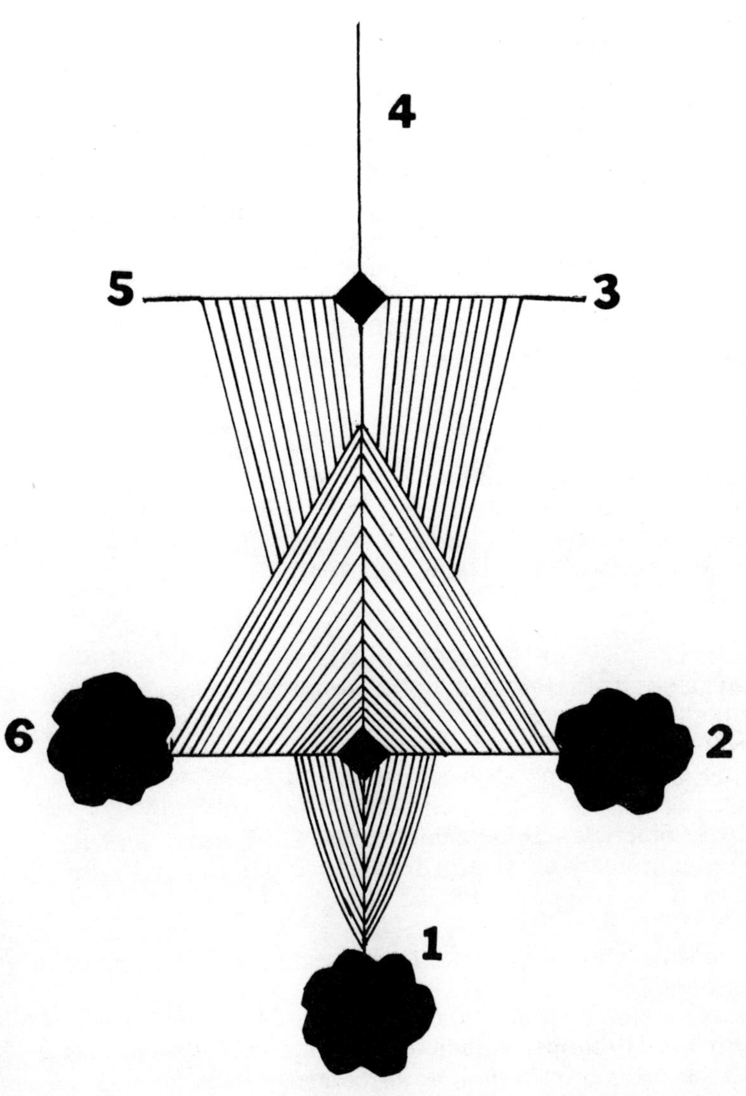

COLOR CHART

1. Unger #9 in shades of rose, or similar bouclé type yarn.
2. Lime green
3. Variegated green mohair
4. Emerald green
5. Green/white nylon craft yarn
6. Moss green
7. Variegated green/white
8. Pink craft raffia
9. Red craft raffia

HOPI PETAL SHIELD

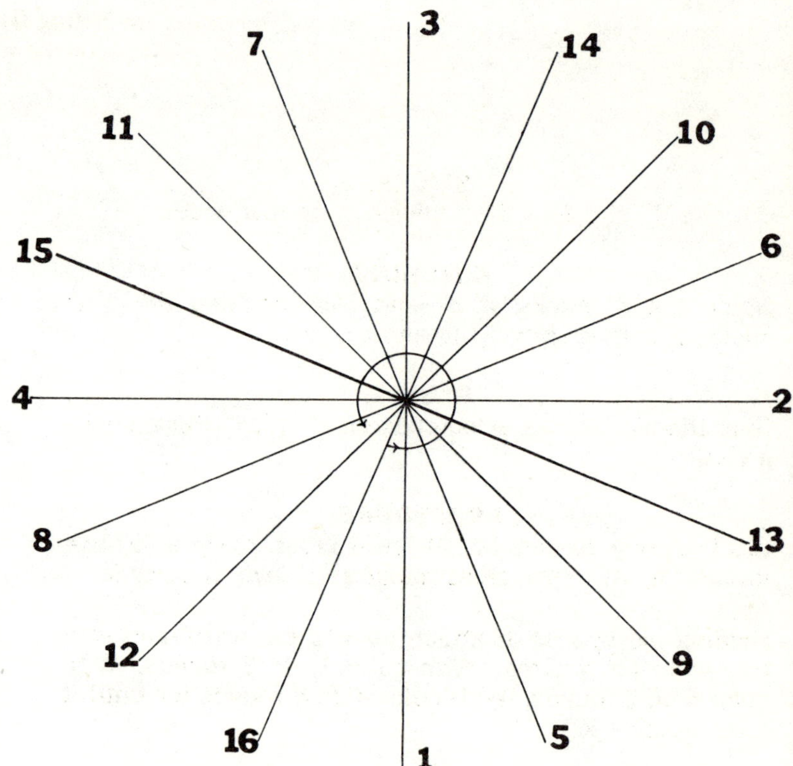

STICKS:

Cut eight sticks 24" long in narrow width.

NOTCHING:

Notch all sticks in center. Bevel ends.

GLUING:

Make four basic ojos by gluing together and let dry. Drill a ⅛" hole through center of each one. Spacing evenly, assemble into a shield by fastening at center with ⅛" screw, 1½" long, secured with nut. Cut off excess screw. Paint sticks dark red.

PROCEDURE:

On back, mark 1½" out on each arm. Placing a dot of glue at each mark, attach color 1 on arm 1 and top wrap every arm for 5 rounds being careful to secure yarn at glue dots.

Begin star wrap by attaching color 2 on arm 1 and top wrapping every other arm (passing under skipped arms) for 4 rounds.

Following star wrap pattern, work colors in following rotation:
Attach color 3 on arm 5, do 4 rounds. Attach color 4 on arm 4, do 4 rounds. Attach color 3 on arm 8, do 4 rounds. Attach color 5 on arm 4, do 4 rounds. Attach color 3 on arm 5, do 4 rounds. Attach color 6 on arm 1, do 4 rounds. Attach color 3 on arm 5, do 4 rounds.

Attach color 2 on arm 3, do 4 rounds. Attach color 3 on arm 14, do 4 rounds. Attach color 4 on arm 1, do 4 rounds. Attach color 3 on arm 5, do 4 rounds. Attach color 5 on arm 12, do 4 rounds. Attach color 3 on arm 16, do 4 rounds. Attach color 3 on arm 3, do 4 rounds.

Attach color 2 on arm 5, do 5 rounds. Attach color 3 on arm 2, do 5 rounds. Attach color 4 on arm 13, do 5 rounds. Attach color 3 on arm 9, do 5 rounds. Attach color 5 on arm 5, do 5 rounds. Attach color 3 on arm 1, do 5 rounds. Attach color 6 on arm 16, do 5 rounds. Attach color 3 on arm 2, do 5 rounds. Attach color 2 on arm 7, do 5 rounds. Attach color 3 on arm 11, do 5 rounds.

Attach color 4 on arm 14, do 5 rounds. Attach color 3 on arm 2, do 5 rounds. Attach color 5 on arm 13, do 5 rounds. Attach color 3 on arm 9, do 5 rounds. Attach color 6 on arm 6, do 5 rounds. Attach color 3 on arm 3, do 5 rounds.

Attach color 1 on arm 5, WRAP EVERY ARM, for 6 rounds.

Attach color 5 on arm 1, IN STAR WRAP, wrap every other arm for 7 rounds. Attach color 5 on arm 13, wrap every other arm for 7 rounds.

FINISHING:

Make a Hopi Sun God (See CENTER TRIMS), using a 2" Prym metal snap button, and red maribou fluff feathers. Fasten on center of ojo. Finish ends by attaching white maribou fluff feathers to each arm. (See HELPFUL HINTS).

COLOR CHART

1. Variegated gray/white/red tweed
2. Pink
3. Medium gray
4. Light rose
5. Bright rose
6. Dark rose

THE POMERANIAN STAR

This ojo is named for the colorful lake district of Poland, an area known for its folklore and embroidered costumes. The Pomeranian region has been called the Polish Switzerland. The stick arangement gives this ojo a quilted appearance.

STICKS:
Cut 4 sticks 14" long, narrow width.

NOTCHING:
Notch each stick in center.

GLUING:
Glue together into 2 basic ojos. When dry, drill a ⅛" hole in center of each cross and put ojos together with a brass screw and nut being sure to space arms evenly.

Paint sticks bright blue.

PROCEDURE:
Attach color 1 on arm 8 and Flower Eye Wrap (See ADVANCED TERMINOLOGY) for 10 rounds.

The rest of the ojo is done in wing wraps throughout.

*With color 2 on arm 1 wing wrap arms 1 and 5 for ¾".
Attach color 14 on arm 2 and wing wrap arms 2 and 6 for ¾".
Attach color 6 on arm 3 and wing wrap arms 3 and 7 for ¾".
Attach color 10 on arm 4 and wing wrap arms 4 and 8 for ¾".
Attach color 3 on arm 1 and wing wrap arms 1 and 5 for ¾".
Attach color 15 on arm 2 and wing wrap arms 2 and 6 for ¾".
Attach color 7 on arm 3 and wing wrap arms 3 and 7 for ¾".
Attach color 11 on arm 4 and wing wrap arms 4 and 8 for ¾".
Attach color 4 on arm 1 and wing wrap arms 1 and 5 for ¾".
Attach color 16 on arm 2 and wing wrap arms 2 and 6 for ¾".
Attach color 8 on arm 3, wing wrap arms 3 and 7 for ¾".
Attach color 12 on arm 4 and wing wrap arms 4 and 8 for ¾".

Repeat from * once.

Attach color 5 on arm 1 and wing wrap arms 1 and 5 for ¾".
Attach color 17 on arm 2 and wing wrap arms 2 and 6 for ¾".
Attach color 9 on arm 3 and wing wrap arms 3 and 7 for ¾".
Attach color 13 on arm 4 and wing wrap arms 4 and 8 for ¾".

Sand the shank off a ¾" wood button, paint blue and glue on center of ojo.

FINISHING:
Obtain a 12" wooden embroidery hoop, available at any knitting or department store. Remove tightening screw and insert a brass jump ring to hold ring together. Paint bright blue. Placing the ring with the opening on the bottom, lay Ojo on top and fasten with glue. Place continuous ring on top being sure it is directly above lower ring and fasten with glue. When dry, hang by inserting small links of chain in jump ring.

COLOR CHART
1. Green/white nylon craft yarn
2. Cream
3. Sunny yellow
4. Orange
5. Rust
6. Light pink
7. Light rose
8. Dark rose
9. Bright red
10. Light lavendar
11. Medium lavendar
12. Dark lavendar
13. Purple
14. Light blue
15. Medium blue
16. Teal blue
17. Copen blue

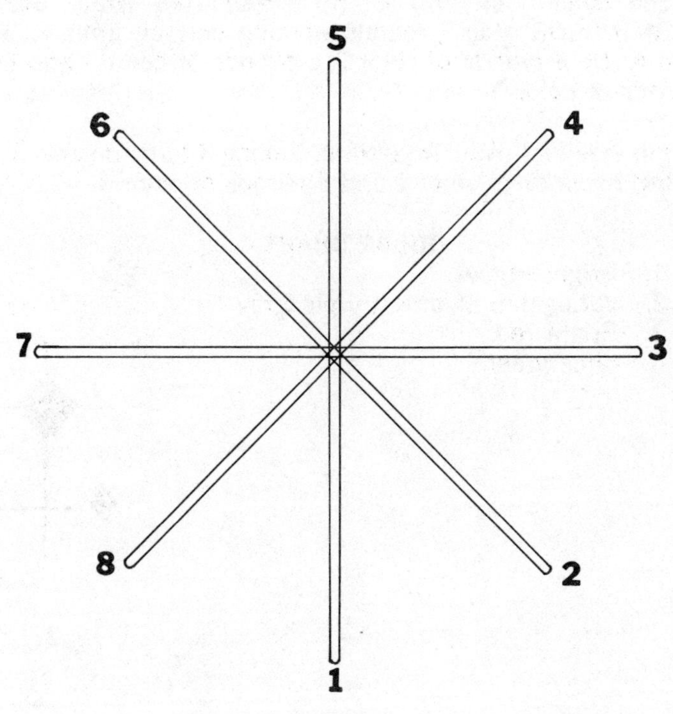

STICKS:
Cut two 24" sticks in narrow width.

NOTCHING:
Notch one stick in center, other one 6½" up from bottom.

GLUING:
Glue sticks together. Paint bright red.

PROCEDURE:
With color 1, make a ½" eye. Top wrap in color 2 for 5 rounds. Do 3 rounds with color 3.
Begin Horizontal Diamond Wrap (See ADVANCED TERMINOLOGY) with color 1 for 5 rounds. Continue diamond wrap with color 4 for 4 rounds. Do not glue off. Extend wrap down arm 1 for ¾".

Attach color 4 on arm 3 and extend wrap for ¾". Do not glue off. Taking one turn around each arm, do 4 rounds in top wrap. Glue off on arm 3.

Attach color 1 on arm 1, do 5 rounds.

Attach color 2 on arm 1. Taking 2 turns around each arm, top wrap for 4 rounds. Do 4 rounds of color 3, 3 rounds of color 4, 3 rounds of color 1 and 3 rounds of color 2, always taking 2 turns around each arm.

Attach color 4 to arm 3. Do 2 rounds. Without gluing off, extend wrap arm 3 for 2". Glue off.

Attach color 4 on arm 2. With Wall Tree Wrap (See TERMINOLOGY) do 7 rounds working only on arms 2, 3 and 4. Do 8 rounds of color 2, 5 rounds of color 4 and 6 rounds of color 3.

Begin extended Wall Tree Wrap, (taking 3 turns on arm 3) doing 7 rounds of color 1 and 5 rounds of color 3.

COLOR CHART
1. Bright yellow
2. Variegated of blue/purple/gray
3. Bright red
4. Lime green

MINI OJO ARM TRIMS

STICKS:
Using either ⅛" dowel or fire place matches, cut 2 pieces 6½" long and 2 pieces 4" long.

NOTCHING:
Notch 4" sticks in center, 6½" sticks 4½" up.

GLUING:
Glue together into two kite shaped ojos and paint sticks bright red.

PROCEDURE:
Using top wrap throughout, do one ojo with a ½" eye in color 1, then 3 rounds of color 2, 3 rounds of color 4 and 6 rounds of color 3. Do second ojo with ½" eye in color 4, 3 rounds of color 3, 3 rounds of color 1 and 6 rounds of color 2.

FINISHING:
Make narrow notches to fit small sticks 1" in from ends of arms 2 and 4 on big ojo. Fasten small ojos so 1½" of long stick is below arms 2 and 4 of big ojo.
Make a 6" French tassel (See MAKING ENDS NEAT) on each side of tree wrap on arms 2 and 4 and attach hanger.

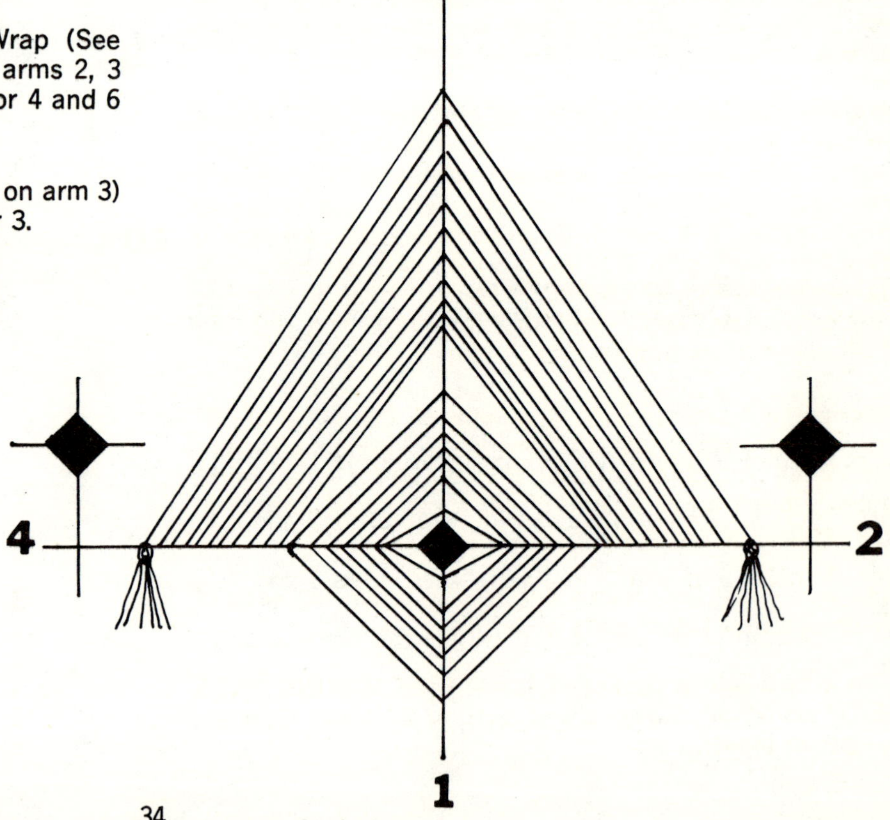

TOLUCA

This ojo was inspired by the swinging braids of the Indian women in Toluca, Mexico, who sell their hand made baskets and art work in the weekly market.

STICKS:

Cut one stick 36" long and 4 sticks 16" long, narrow width.

NOTCHING:

Notch 16" sticks in center. Notch 36" stick at 5", 13", 21" and 29" up from bottom.

GLUING:

Glue 16" sticks at notches. Paint sticks bright yellow.

PROCEDURE:

OJO #1 — With color 1 do a 1" eye. With color 4, do a figure 8 top wrap for 2 patterns (See TERMINOLOGY). With color 5, backwrap for ¾". With color 2, figure 8 top wrap for 3 complete patterns.

OJO #2 — With color 2 make a 1" eye. With color 5 do a figure 8 top wrap for 2 patterns. With color 6, backwrap for ¾". With color 4, figure 8 top wrap for 3 complete rounds.

OJO #3 — With color 3, do a 1" eye. With color 1, do a figure 8 top wrap for 2 patterns. With color 2, backwrap for ¾". With color 5, figure 8 top wrap for 3 complete patterns.

OJO #4 — With color 4 do a 1" eye. With color 2 do a figure 8 top wrap for 2 patterns. With color 1, backwrap for ¾". With color 6, do a Wall Tree Wrap (See ADVANCED TERMINOLOGY) for 10 rounds, gluing off on arm 3 after returning from arm 4. Trim with 3 rows of color 4.

BRAIDS: Using 1 strand of each color, cut 6 groups 46" long. Knot each group together with simple overhand knot 2" from one end. Separate groups into 3 strands, placing 3 on each side of top cross arms and fastening snugly under the arm with a square knot. Arrange 3 groups on each side 3½" from ends. With simple braiding, work to within 4" of end. Fasten all strands with one simple overhand knot. Tack to each cross arm with dot of glue and allow bottom end to hang freely.

Unwrapped tassels: Cut 24 groups of the 6 colors, 9" long. Knot each group 2" from ends with simple overhand knot. Attaching in same manner as for long braids, fasten groups on each side of each horizontal arm 1" in from ends. Do not braid.

With wire brush (such as a pet brush), brush top ends of all groups and tassel ends of braids.

Trim arm 6 with a cockaded tassel (See MAKING ENDS NEAT) using all 6 colors and cutting 6" long. Conceal hanger in tassel.

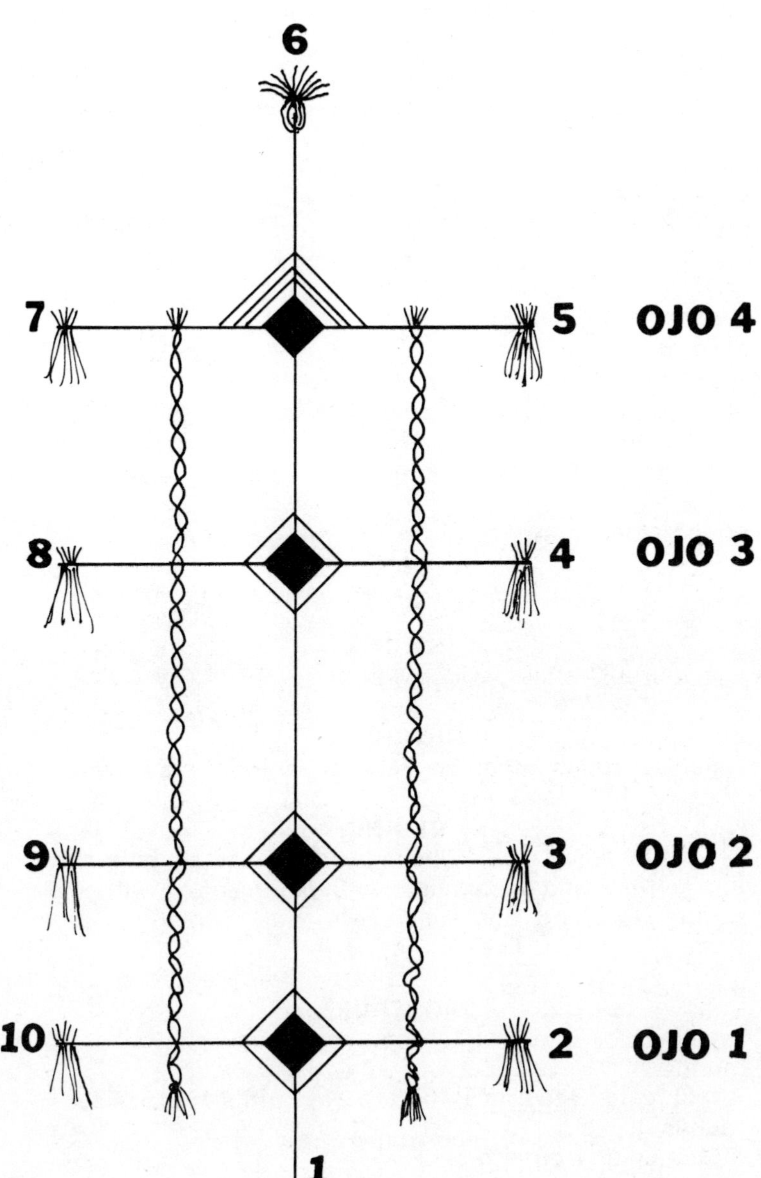

COLOR CHART

1. Tweed in shades of green/cream/yellow
2. Orange
3. Golden brown
4. Medium green
5. White
6. Lime green

VIKING SHIELD

(Shield Ojo)

COLOR CHART
1. Bright yellow
2. Royal blue
3. Medium blue
4. Cream
5. Teal blue

STICKS:

Cut four 18" sticks, wide width.

NOTCHING:

Notch all sticks in center. Bevel ends. Paint sticks white.

GLUING:

Glue into basic ojos. When dry drill a small hole thru the centers and fasten into a 8 point shield with 1/8" screw, 1½" long, and secure with nut. Screw will protrude (DO NOT CUT OFF).

PROCEDURE:

Attach color 1 to arm 1. Top wrap arms 1, 2, 3, 4 for 6 rounds.
Attach color 2 to arm 1 and top wrap arms 1, 2, 3, 4 for 4 rounds.
Attach color 1 on arm 5.

Wrap over arms 2 and 6, around 6, over arms 3 and 7, around 7. Over arms 4 and 8, around 8, over arms 1 and 5 around 5 for 5 rounds. Attach color 2 on arm 5 and repeat from.

Attach color 3 to arm 1. Top wrap each arm in succession for 4 rounds.
Attach color 4 to arm 1. Top wrap each arm in succession for 3 rounds.
Attach color 5 to arm 1. Top wrap each arm in succession for 3 rounds.

Attach color 1 to arm 3. Back wrap for 7 rounds.

Attach color 3 to arm 3. Wing wrap arms 3 and 1 for ¾".
Attach color 3 to arm 4. Wing wrap arms 4 and 2 for ¾".

Attach color 3 on arm 3. **Go over arm 3, under and around arm 7, over and around arm 4, under and around arm 8, over and around arm 1, under and around arm 5, over and around arm 2, under and around arm 6, and over arm 3. Do 6 rounds.

Attach color 2 on arm 1. Wing wrap arms 1 and 3 for ½".
Attach color 2 on arm 4. Wing wrap arms 4 and 2 for ½".

Attach color 4 on arm 3. Repeat the ** wrapping for 6 rounds.

Taking 2 turns each time, attach color 2 on arm 1 and wing wrap arms 1 and 3 for 1". Attach color 2 on arm 2, and wing wrap arms 2 and 4 for 1".

Attach color 5 on arm 3. Repeating the ** directions and taking 2 turns on arms 1, 2, 3 and 4, and 1 turn on arms 5, 6, 7 and 8, do 6 rounds.

Attach color 1 on arm 4. Back wrap working only on arms 3, 2, 1, and 4 for 6 rounds. Change to top wrap and do 5 rounds continuing to work only on arms 1, 2, 3 and 4.

Attach color 2 on arm 4. Taking 2 turns on each arm, top wrap 4 rounds working only on arms 1, 2, 3 and 4. Taking only 1 turn on each arm do 2 rounds.

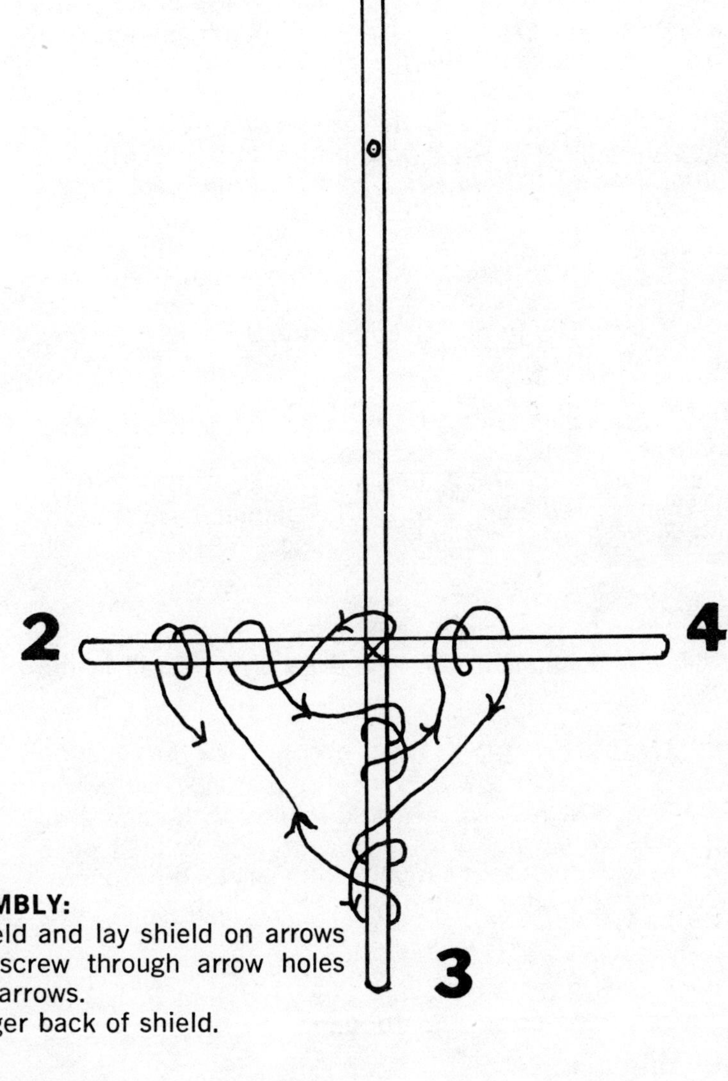

VIKING SHIELD (ARROWS)

STICKS:
Cut two 6" sticks, narrow width. Cut two 36" and two 12" sticks in wide width.

NOTCHING:
Notch 36" sticks 7" up for a wide stick, and 32½" up for a narrow stick. Notch the 4 shorter sticks in center. Drill a ⅛" hole 21¾" up the 36" stick. Placing the 36" stick on template and matching the screw holes, notch for a 50⁰ angle. Bevel all ends. Paint sticks white.

GLUING:
Glue the two 12" sticks at the 7" notch. Wait until arrowheads have been wrapped before gluing smaller sticks at 32½" notch.

PROCEDURE:
ARROWHEAD #1: (Be sure wrap is on same side as diagonal notch).
NOTE: — The arrowheads are done in Wall Tree Wrap (See ADVANCED TERMINOLOGY). Always glue on arm 2 and off on arm 4.

With color 2, do a half-eye for 1½". With color 1 do 3 rounds. With color 3 do 4 rounds. With color 4 do 4 rounds. With color 5 do 5 rounds. With color 1 do 5 rounds. With color 2 do 5 rounds. With color 3 do 3 rounds. With color 4 do 3 rounds. With color 2 do 6 rounds.

ARROWHEAD #2: (Be sure wrap is on opposite side as diagonal notch.)
Make a matching arrowhead to #1.

ARROW NOCK ENDS: (Always glue on and off on arms 2A)
With color 3, do an eye that measures ¾" on long side. (Because of different wood widths, eye will be diamond-shaped).

With color 1, wing wrap arms 2A and 4A for 6 rounds. With color 2, do 2 rounds wing wrap for trim.

With color 5 on arm 3A, backwrap for ¾". Without gluing off, place 3 color 5 feathers on nock ends and wrap securely.

ASSEMBLY:
Carefully remove nut on shield and lay shield on arrows at 21¾" notching. Fasten screw through arrow holes and tighten nut on back of arrows.
Hang by attaching yarn hanger back of shield.

MEDICINE MAN

STICKS:

Cut one 20", one 24", and one 45" stick in wide width.

NOTCHING:

Notch 45" stick 10" up and 26" up. Notch other two sticks in center.

GLUING:

Glue the 20" stick at 10" notch, and the 24" stick at the 26" notch. Arrow all ends. Stain with dark wood stain.

PROCEDURE:

LOWER CROSS:

With color 1, do a 1" eye. With color 2 do 5 rounds, with color 3 do 5 rounds, with color 4 do 6 rounds, with color 1 do 2 rounds, all in top wrap.

Attach color 5 on arm 2. Wall Tree Wrap (See ADVANCED TERMINOLOGY) for 6 rounds. With color 1 do 4 rounds, with color 2 do 5 rounds, with color 3 do 5 rounds, with color 4 do 6 rounds, with color 5 do 5 rounds, with color 1 do 6 rounds, with color 4 do 3 rounds, with color 3 do 7 rounds, all in Wall Tree Wrap.

Attach color 2 on arm 1, and extend wrap for 2". Without gluing off, top wrap from arm 1 to arm 2 with 1½ turns, to arm 1 then to arm 6 with 1½ turns, back to arm 1. Continue for 3 complete rounds.

Attach color 1 to arm 1 with cut end toward right (arm 6). Wind over arm 6 with 1½ turns, over arm 1, over arm 2 with 1½ turns. Continue for 3 complete turns, gluing off on arm 1.

Attach color 4 on arm 6. Using same wall tree wrap, do 3 complete rounds.
Attach color 3 on arm 2, continuing same wall tree wrap, do 1" measured along arm 2. This should leave approximately 1" of arms 2 and 6 unwrapped.

UPPER CROSS:

With color 1, do a 1" eye. With color 2 do 4 rounds, with color 3 do 4 rounds, with color 4 do 5 rounds all in top wrap.

FROM NOW ON, DO 2 WRAPS ON EACH ARM. With color 5 do 6 rounds, with color 3 do 5 rounds, with color 1 do 3 rounds, with color 4 do 6 rounds, with color 2 do 5 rounds, with color 1 do 4 rounds, with color 3 do 6 rounds, with color 5 do 4 rounds, with color 4 do 3 rounds. Wrapping only once around each arm, attach color 3 and do 7 rounds.

Attach color 2 on arm 5. Wall tree wrap arms 5, 4, 3 for 6 rounds. With color 1 do 4 rounds.

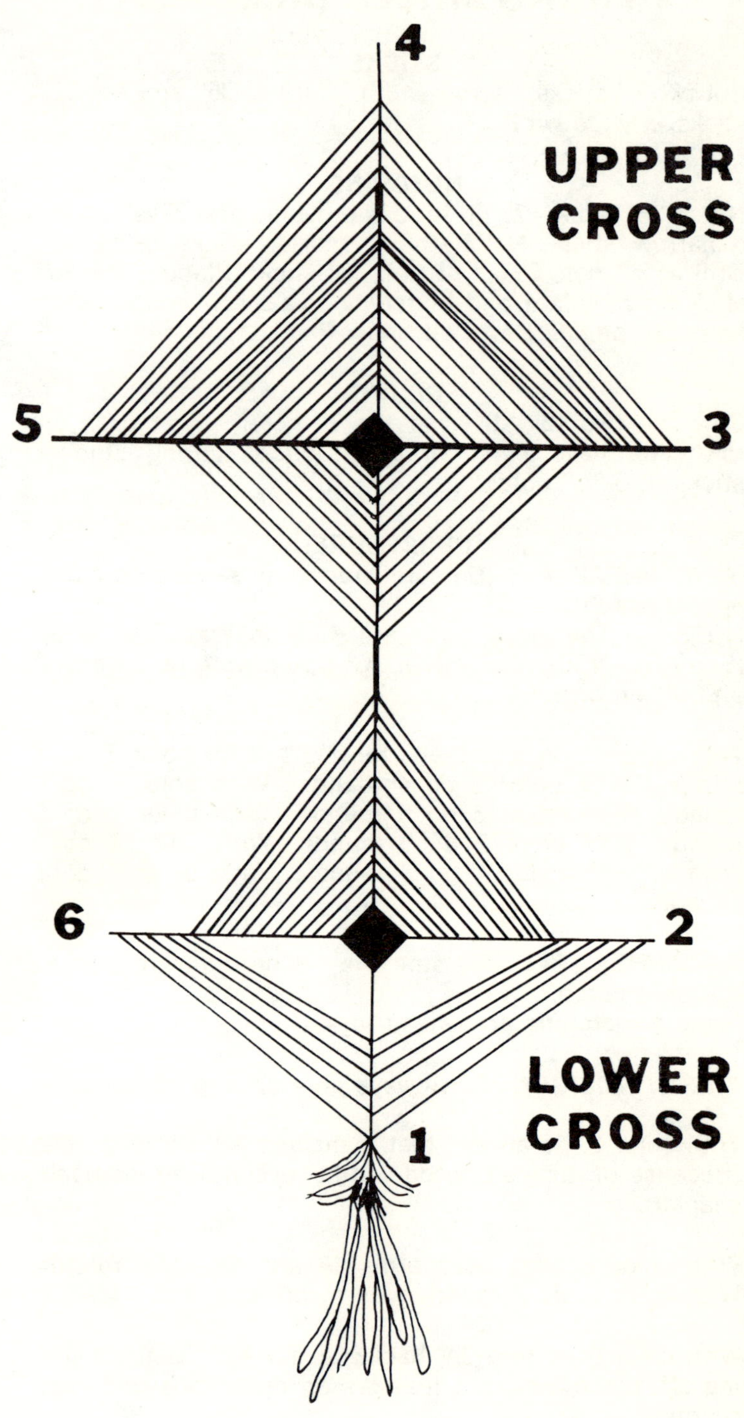

With color 1 extend wrap arm 4 for 1¾".

Begin space wall tree wrap with 2 turns on arm 4.
Attach color 4 on arm 3 (always glue off on arm 5). Do 5 rounds. Attach color 3 on arm 3 and do 4 rounds. Attach color 5 on arm 3 and do 2 rounds. Attach color 1 on arm 3 and do 2 rounds. This should all be space wall tree wrap.

Taking only 1 turn around each arm, attach color 3 on arm 3 and do 7 rounds.

FINISHING:
Space 6 eagle-type feathers (12" long), in white with black tips, around a small cork. Fasten into cork with straight pins. Cut an oblong opening in top of cork, force on arm 1 and glue. With color 2, wind yarn on arm 1 and down to bottom of cork. Carefully glue 6 or 8 small red maribou feathers to cover junction of arm 1 and cork and wind upper ends with a few turns of color 2.
For additional trim, fasten 2 groups of 3 small feathers (one red, one black, and one white) together by winding upper quills with color 3, tie to upper left and upper right of top ojo at different heights.

Fasten a loop hanger in upper cross.

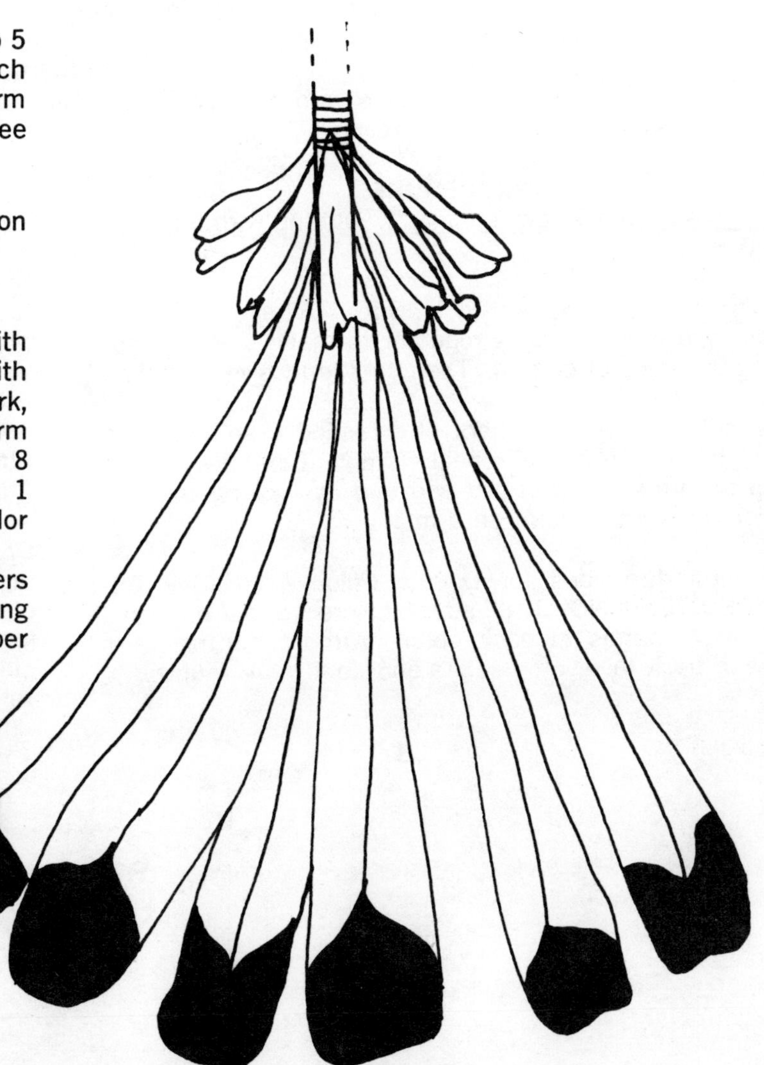

COLOR CHART
1. Red sparkle
2. Variegated gray/white/black
3. Black
4. White
5. Medium gray

SNOWFLAKE

(Wall hanging — Ojo A)

STICKS:
Cut four 18" sticks in narrow width.

NOTCHING:
Notch each stick in center. Bevel ends.

GLUING:
Glue into two basic 18" ojos and paint sticks bright green.

PROCEDURE:
On Ojo #1, do a 1" eye in color 1. Outline with 5 rounds of color 2.

On Ojo #2, top wrap with color 3 for 1¾" eye. Spacing evenly, put ojos together to make shield shape using 3 rounds of color 4. Then do 3 rounds in color 5.

With color 6, *wrap 6 rounds of extended wrap on arm 1, move to next arm and repeat from *. Continue around until all arms are wrapped and end by tucking the end under the starting yarn on arm 1.

Following directions for Double Color Wrap (See ADVANCED TERMINOLOGY), attach colors 3 and 7 on arm 1 and do 4 rounds in each color. Without cutting yarn, twist in back to reverse colors and do 4 more rounds.

Attach color 4 to arm 7 and do 2 rounds of top wrap. With color 2 on arm 1, do Star Wrap (See TERMINOLOGY) for 10 rounds. With color 4 on arm 3, top wrap each arm for 2 rounds. With color 6 on arm 5, Star Wrap for 10 rounds. With color 4 on arm 1, do 2 rounds top wrapping each arm.

Attach color 5 on arm 5 and do 10 rounds of back wrap. Attach color 1 on arm 6 and do 6 rounds of back wrap. Attach color 6 on arm 1 and Star Wrap for 11 rounds. Attach color 6 on arm 5 and Star Wrap for 11 rounds.

On bottom of arm 1, attach feather tassel by doing macramé knots on 3 large ceramic beads, using two strands of color 6 for holding cords, and two strands of color 2 for tying cords. (See Diagram in NIGHT OWL). Wrap quills of 4 large feathers placed so they curve outward with ends of yarn. To attach, drill small hole in arm 1, ¼" from end, pull the 4 strands of yarn through and tie a finger knot behind the hole.

**FOR OJO PLACEMENT,
REFER TO DIAGRAM PAGE 44.**

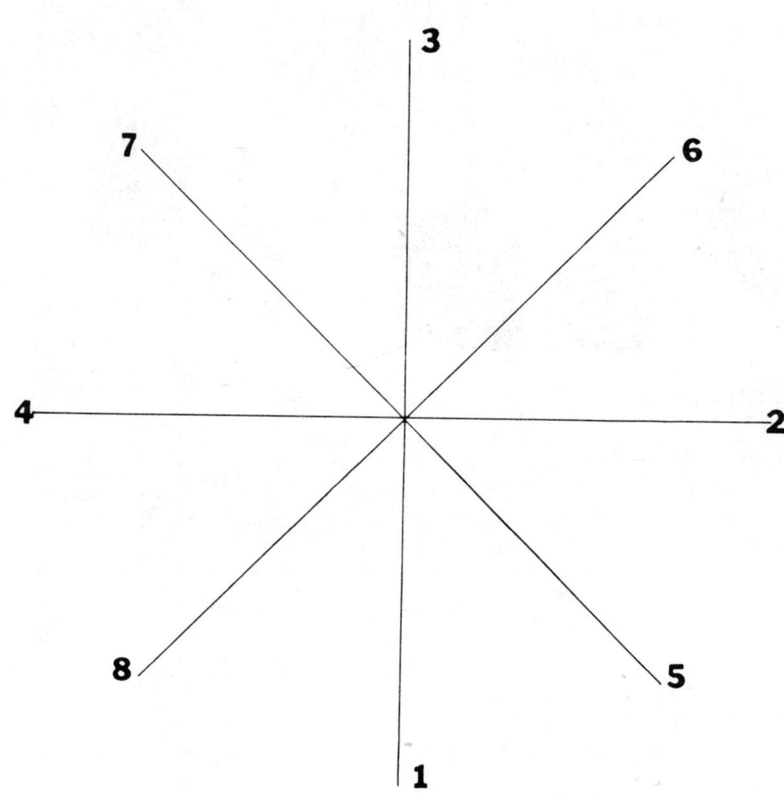

COLOR CHART
1. Bucilla multi in yellow/orange
2. Light orange
3. Lime green
4. Unger #9 or similar bouclé-type yarn in shades of green/cream
5. Hot pink
6. Moss green
7. Golden yellow

FIRST STAR

(Wall Hanging — Ojo B)

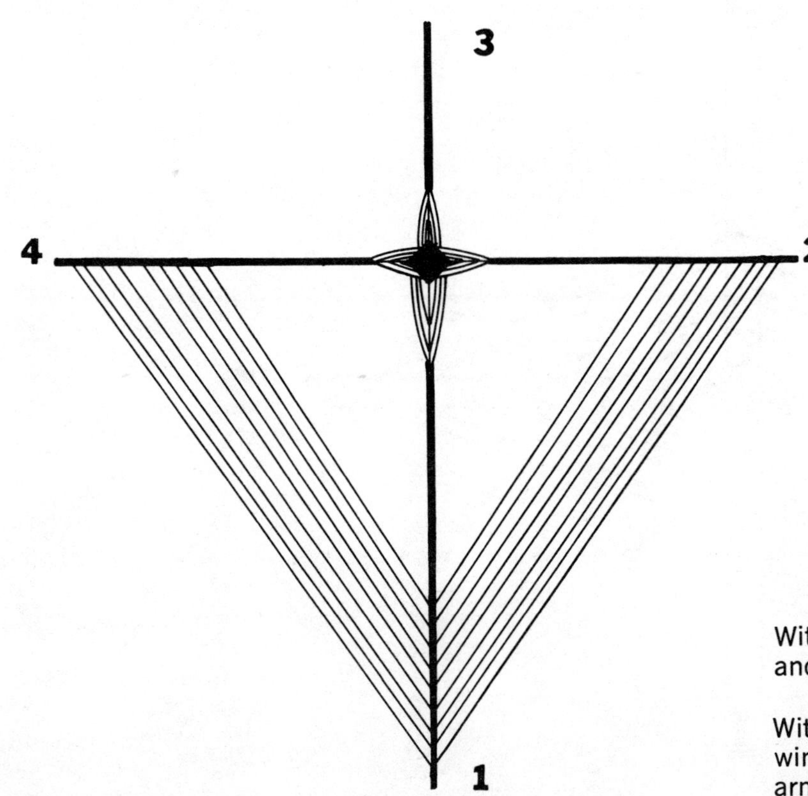

STICKS:

Cut one 24" and one 18" stick, narrow width.

NOTCHING:

Notch 18" stick in center, 24" stick 10" down from top. Bevel ends.

GLUING:

Glue sticks together at notches. Paint bright green.

PROCEDURE:

With color 1, make a ¾" eye. Outline with one round of color 2.

With color 3, do ½" wing wraps on arms 1 and 3, and 2 and 4, adding one round of color 2 to finish each wing wrap.

With color 4, do ½" wing wrap on arms 1 and 3, and 2 and 4, again trimming with one round color 2.

With color 5, do ½" wing wrap on arms 1 and 2, and 2 and 4, trimming each wing with one round color 2.

With color 6, do a 1" wing wrap on arms 1 and 3 and 2 and 4, trimming each wing with one round color 2.

With color 7, glue on behind arm 1. Do an elongated wing wrap on arms 1 and 3 only by taking 2 turns around arm 1 and one turn around arm 3. Work until wrap on arm 1 is 1" and trim with one round of color 2. Glue off.

Holding ojo by arm 3, put a dot of glue 3½" from ends of arms 2 and 4 and 6" from end of arm 1. Attach color 1 behind arm 2. Using DOUBLE TREE wrap (See ADVANCED TERMINOLOGY) do four complete wraps. Glue off on arm 2.

Attach color 4 behind arm 2. Continuing in DOUBLE TREE wrap, do 3 complete rounds and glue off. With color 2, do one complete round. With color 5 on arm 2, do 3 complete rounds. With color 6 on arm 2, do 5 complete rounds.

Measure off 36" of color 7 and glue on arm 2. String 20 small orange beads (3/16" diameter) on yarn. Spacing 10 evenly on each side, do one round and glue off.

COLOR CHART

1. Hot pink
2. Unger or similar bouclé-type yarn in variegated green
3. Variegated yellow
4. Moss
5. Orange
6. Lime
7. Yellow

SAGITTARIA

(Wall Hanging — Ojo C)

Sagittaria is a plant with arrowhead-shaped leaves.

STICKS:
Cut one 15″ and one 18″ stick narrow width.

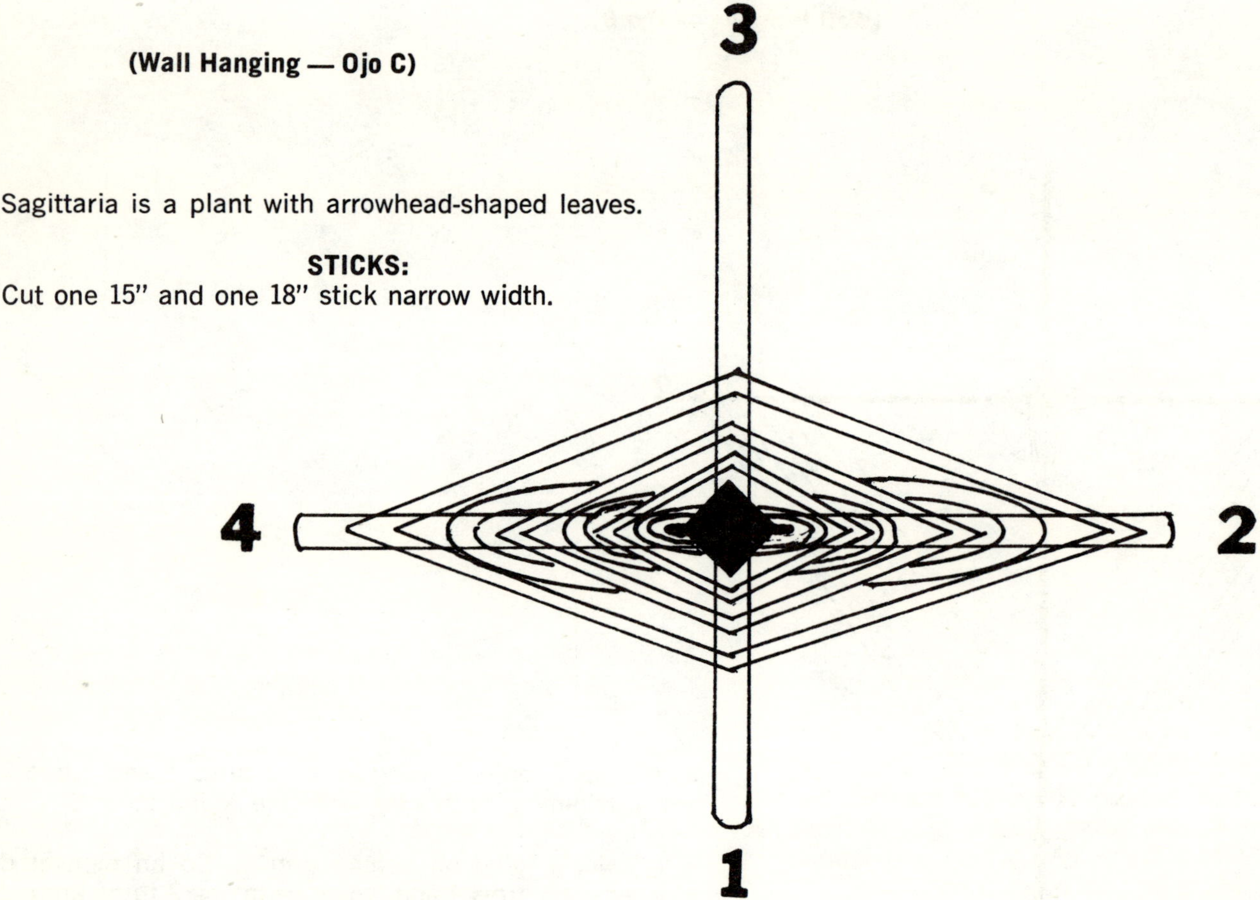

NOTCHING:
Notch the 18″ stick in center and the 15″ stick 6″ from bottom. Bevel ends.

GLUING:
Glue sticks together at notches and paint bright green.

PROCEDURE:

With color 1, do a 1¼″ eye in top wrap.

Wing wrap on arms 2 and 4 in color 2 for ¾″.

With color 3, back wrap for 11 rounds.

With color 4, do 3 rounds of top wrap.

Wing wrap on arms 2 and 4 in color 2 for ¾″.

With color 3, back wrap for 6 rounds.

With color 4, do 2 rounds of top wrap.

Wing wrap on arms 2 and 4 in color 2 for ¾″.

With color 3, back wrap for 11 rounds.

With color 4, do 2 rounds of top wrap.

Wing wrap on arms 2 and 4 in color 2 for ¾″.

With color 3, back wrap for 9 rounds.

Finish with 3 rounds of color 4 in top wrap.

Leave arms untrimmed.

COLOR CHART
1. Moss green
2. Hot pink
3. Lime green
4. Unger #9, or similar bouclé-type yarn in shades of green/cream.

TEARDROP

(Wall hanging — Ojo D)

STICKS:
Cut one 16" and one 24" stick narrow width.

NOTCHING:
Notch 16" stick in center and 24" stick 7½" down. Bevel ends.

GLUING:
Glue together at notches and paint bright green.

PROCEDURE:
With color 1, make an eye of 4 rounds. Now start 2 wraps on arms 2 and 4, 1 on arm 3, and 3 on arm 1 and do 6 rounds. Glue off on 2nd turn of arm 1.

Attach color 2 on arm 1. Using same space wrap, do 4 rounds ending with 2 wraps on arm 1.

Attach color 3 on arm 1. * Begin figure 8 wrap by going over arm 1, under arm 2 and back under arm 1; Over the top from behind arm 2; Over the top of arm 1 from behind; under arm 2 and around; Over arm 3, back over arm 2, back over arm 3, back over arm 2. Around arm 3, behind and around arm 4, behind and around arm 3, behind and around arm 4, behind and around arm 3, behind and around arm 4, over and around arm 1, over and around arm 4, over and around arm 1, over and around arm 4, over and around arm 1. Repeat from*.

With color 4, do one complete pattern in figure 8 wrap. With color 5, wrap arm 1 down 5". Attach color 6 on arm 2; then go over arm 2,** over and around arm 3, over and around arm 4 (work entirely on front side), back over and around arm 3, over and around arm 2. Repeat from ** for 1".

Attach color 7 on arm 1. Top wrap covering all arms in succession for 9 rounds being careful to keep threads flat.

Attach color 5 on arm 4, Wall Tree Wrap (See ADVANCED TERMINOLOGY) on arms 4, 1, 2 for 7 rounds. Attach color 4 on arm 3 and top wrap all arms in succession for 3 rounds.

Attach color 8 on arm 2, back wrap each arm in succession for 8 rounds. Attach color 3 on arm 2. Using Wall Tree Wrap work arms 2, 3, and 4 for 7 rounds. Finish with 1 round of color 4 on arms 2, 3, and 4 only.

Attach color 6 on arm 4. Using Wall Tree Wrap, take 2 turns around arm 4, 2 turns around arm 1, 1½ turns around arm 2, 2 turns around arm 1, 1½ turns around arm 4, 2 turns around arm 1, 1½ turns around arm 4.

Continuing with this space tree wrap, work 6 rounds ending on arm 2. Finish with 1 round of color 4 working only arms 4, 1 and 2.

Turn ojo so arm 1 is at top. Fasten a small screw eye to arms 2, 3, and 4. Attach plastic tear drop jewels (used for craft lamp making) to a small brass jump ring inserted in screw eye.

COLOR CHART
1. Golden brown
2. Peach
3. Lime green
4. Unger #9 in green/cream, or similar bouclé yarn.
5. Light orange
6. Golden yellow
7. Moss green
8. Hot pink

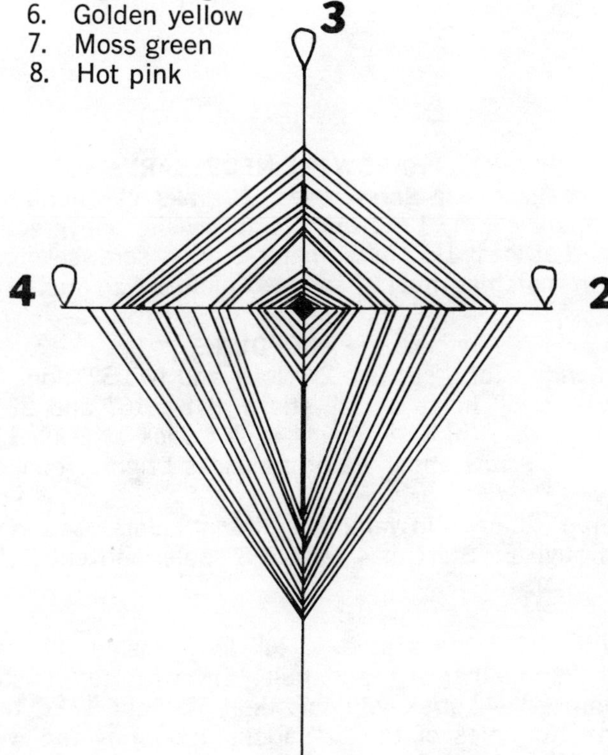

WALL HANGING – Trims and Finishing

PROCEDURE:

Make a pair of matching mini ojos as follows:

Cut narrow width sticks, two 4" and two 7" long. Notch in center. Bevel ends. Glue together and paint bright green.

With color 1, do ½" eye; outline with 2 rows of color 2. Attach color 7 and Vertical Diamond wrap (See AD-VANCED TERMINOLOGY) for 3 rounds. With color 3 Vertical Diamond Wrap for 4 rounds. With color 4, Vertical Diamond wrap for 2 rounds. With color 5, Vertical Diamond wrap for 2 rounds. With color 6, top wrap for 3 rounds. Trim with one round top wrap of color 2.

COLOR CHART

1. Bright orange
2. Unger #9 or similar bouclé-type yarn in shades of green/cream
3. Moss green
4. Bucilla multi in yellow/orange
5. Hot pink
6. Lime green
7. Golden brown

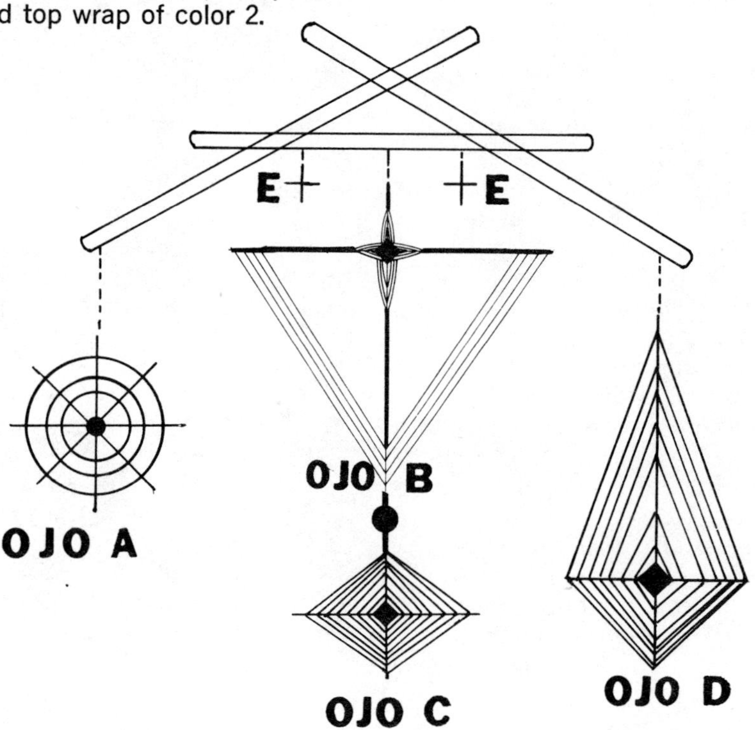

HARDWARE NECESSARY:

7 smallest size screw eyes, 21 links of anodized gold drapery chain, 3 teardrop lamp jewels, one green wood bead at least 1½" in diameter, 3 brass screws ¾" x 3/16" with matching nuts, 2 serrated picture hangers.

PROCEDURE:

In wide width, cut one 24" long and two 32" long sticks. Drill 3/16" holes in 32" sticks at 8", 16" and 27" from one end. Drill 3/16" holes in 24" stick at 6¼", 12" and 17¾". Arrow ends. Paint all sticks bright green.

Wrap 32" stick in varying widths of colors used in ojos A through E. Start at 4" above 8" hole, and end ½" from 27" hole.

With 3/16" brass screws, ¾" long, fasten the two 32" sticks together at the 8" hole. End with nut. Fasten un-wrapped 24" stick with screws at 6¼" and 17¾" holes to the 16" holes of the 32" sticks, mounting the wrapped sticks on top. Fasten with nuts.

Using drapery chain, put one link through each of the 27" holes on the 32" stick, and one at the center hole on the 24" stick.

Screw small screw eyes in top of ojos E. Also insert screw eyes in bottom edge of 24" stick, 4" each side of center hole. Attach ojos E to the screw eyes in 24" stick with one link of drapery chain.

Drill a 3/16" hole in arm 3 of ojos A, B, C and D ⅜" from ends. Also drill same hole in arm 1 of ojo B. Put a drapery chain link in each hole.

With 3 links of drapery chain, attach ojos A and D (making a total of 5 links). With one link, attach ojo B (making a total of 3 links). Run 3 links through the center of a large green wood bead at least 1½" in diameter, squeezing links if necessary, and attach ojo C to ojo B.

Hang by attaching two serrated picture hangers on 24" stick directly above ojos E.

TABLE TOP OJO

All ojos do not have to be made from pieces of wood or wire. It is possible to make ojos of items already manufactured. For instance, an ojo can be made on a small bicycle wheel, a clock with projecting radiating arms, etc. In this instance, the ojo was made on a small spinning wheel which was designed as a table top planter. It could also be adapted to a full sized spinning wheel. Made in centennial colors, the early American design fits nicely into any decor.

For ease of working, the wheel was carefully removed from the planter (which came from a trading stamp company) and then replaced after winding.

PROCEDURE:

With color 1, do double wrap (See ADVANCED TERMINOLOGY) for 3 rounds.

Attach color 2, in the usual way, color 3 in the reverse way (with cut end toward right). In spectrum wrap (See ADVANCED TERMINOLOGY), do 1 round. Reversing colors, do 1 round. Reversing colors, do 1 more round.

With color 4 do double wrap for 3 rounds (be sure to finish third round on back before gluing off.)

With color 5, do 2 rounds double wrap. With color 2, 2 rounds of double wrap.

Gluing color 3 in usual way, and color 1 in reverse way, do 2 rounds in spectrum wrap.

With color 5 double wrap for 3 rounds. With color 3, double wrap for 4 rounds. With color 1, double wrap for 3 rounds. With color 2, double wrap for 3 rounds. With color 5, double wrap for 2 rounds.

Threading color 2 in a yarn needle, finish out with 2 rounds of double wrap being sure to complete both sides.

These directions will complete an 8½" wheel.

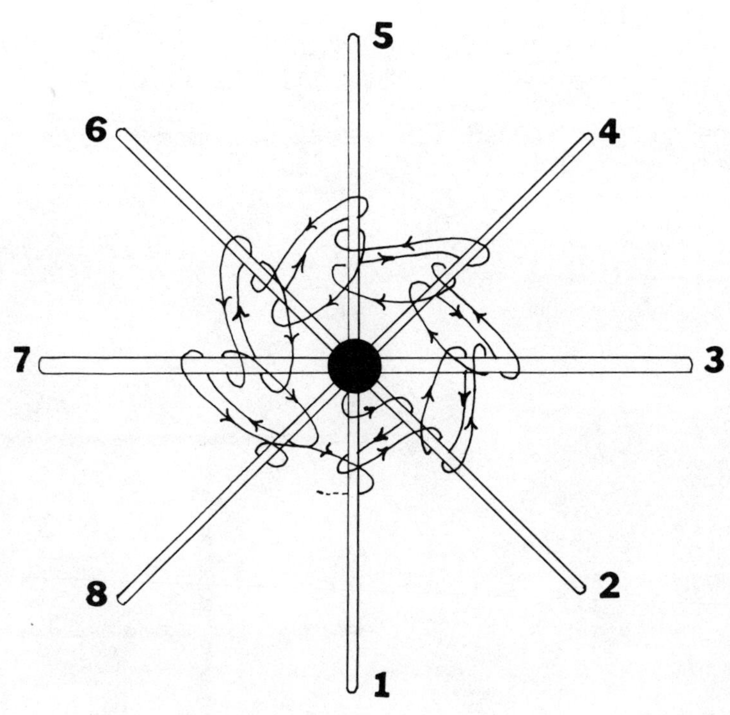

COLOR CHART
1. Royal blue
2. Variegated red/white/blue mohair
3. Warm rose
4. Light blue
5. White bouclé

ROOM DIVIDER

Base

This unit is made of precut component parts, available in most building materials centers. With no cutting required, and with many different parts offered, it can be made any size, any height, any style.

First decide whether you want it to be a free-standing divider, or one that reaches floor to ceiling with tension adjusters at top. Then plan the basic ojo design you wish to use. Any of the ojos in this book may be adapted, even some of the mobile type, by simply changing the dimensions (See DESIGNING AN OJO). Most dividers will be easier to make when unit is completely assembled.

For the one pictured, the following component parts were used:

    Four 16" legs in Colonial style
    One 36" x 10" shelf
    Six acorn finials
    Two 48" spindles for upright sides
    Two spacers for locking on spindles
    Two metal connector kits

The unit was stained with nutmeg stain and finished with satin varnish.

Ojo Frame

STICKS:

Cut three 36" and two 35" sticks in wide width. Cut one 37¾", two 13" and two 5" sticks in narrow width.

NOTCHING:

Notch one 36" stick in center to fit narrow stick. Notch two 36" sticks in center to fit narrow stick and also 8" in from each end to fit wide stick.

Notch 37¾" narrow stick 27¾" up to fit wide stick. MARK, DO NOT NOTCH AT 18" UP.

Notch two 35" wide sticks up from bottom at 10½", 13" to fit narrow stick and at 27½" up from bottom to fit wide stick.

These were also stained in nutmeg and varnished.

All notching must be done before the sticks are stained and before assembly. The assembly should be done before staining, then any touchup needed may be added later.

Marking every 1½" above the 27¾" notch on long narrow stick, drill small hole to accommodate barbeque skewer stick. Make six holes. BE SURE TO DRILL SO STICKS INSERTED IN HOLES WILL RUN IN SAME DIRECTION AS HORIZONTAL OJO STICKS. Refer to diagram on page 49.
Assemble sticks as diagrammed.

Fasten frame to room divider base before wrapping.

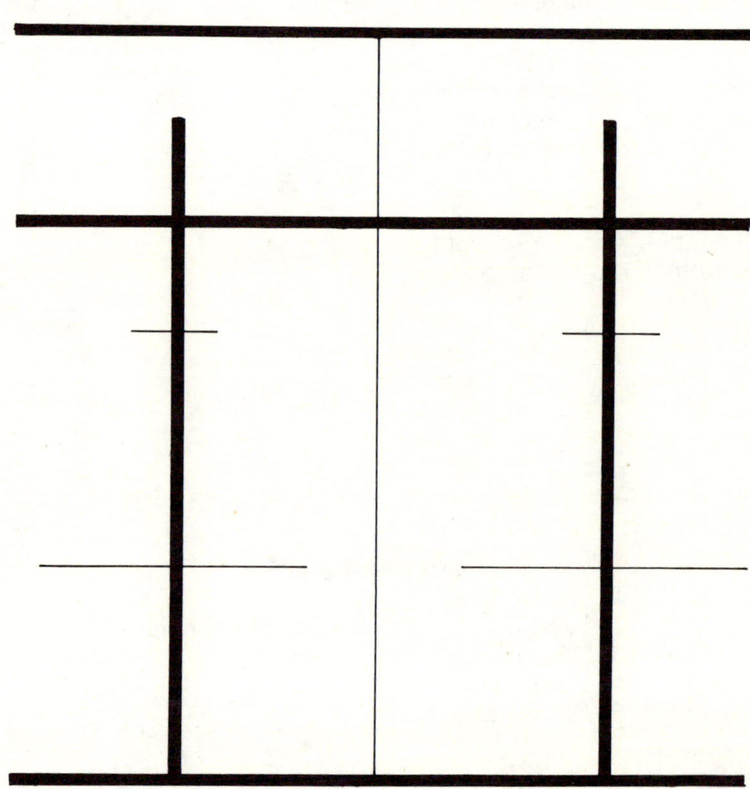

ROOM DIVIDER

PINWHEEL

The frame for this ojo was made of welding rod, welded in center and shaped as shown in diagram. It may also be made of heavy coat hanger wire, either welded in center or glued with an adhesive such as Epoxy. Enlarge the diagram below fitting it into a 12" circle.

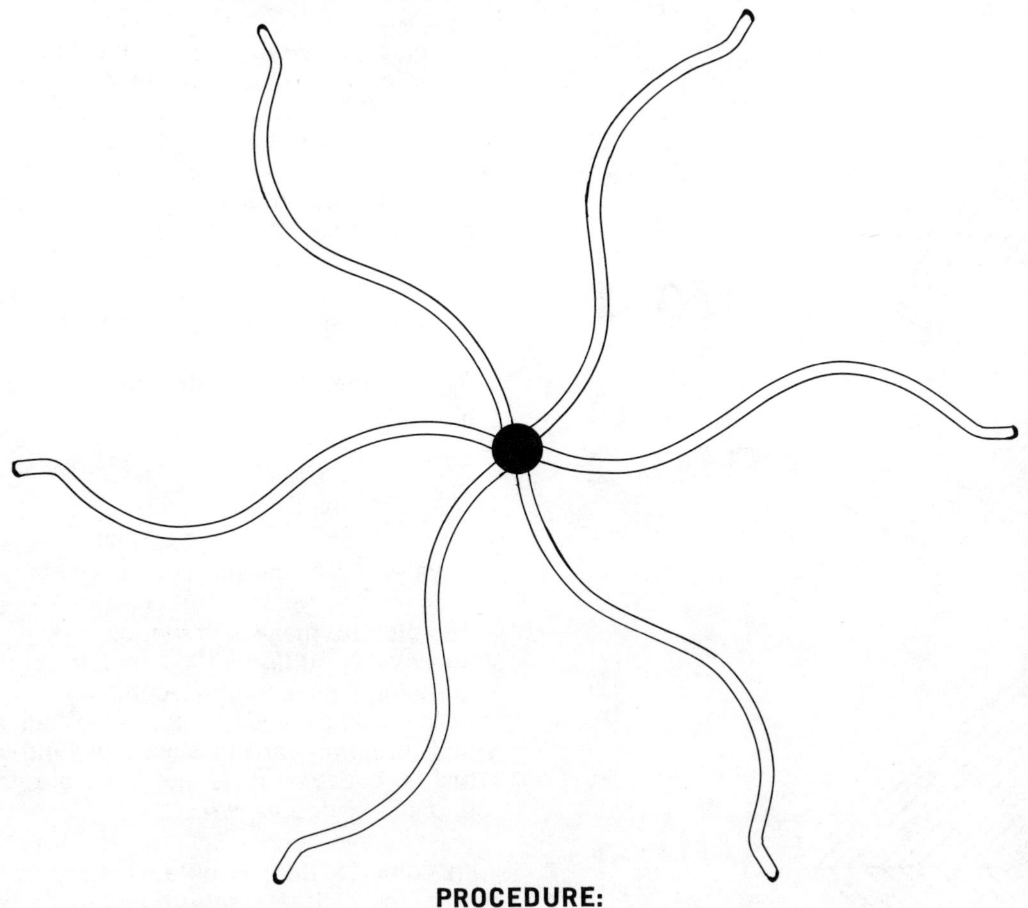

PROCEDURE:
With color 1, do 6 rounds of top wrap to cover center. (A small circle will not be covered and if brazed will be a pleasing gold color).

FROM NOW ON, ENTIRE OJO IS BACK WRAPPED.
With color 2, do 3 rounds
With color 3, do 4 rounds
With color 4, do 5 rounds
With color 2, do 2 rounds
With color 1, do 5 rounds
With color 5, do 7 rounds
With color 3, do 3 rounds
With color 2, do 3 rounds
With color 4, do 5 rounds
With color 1, do 6 rounds
With color 6, do 5 rounds
With color 2, do 3 rounds
With color 3, do 4 rounds

Make a Second ojo to match, working on opposite side so shaping will match exactly when placed back to back.

ROOM DIVIDER

TRILOGY

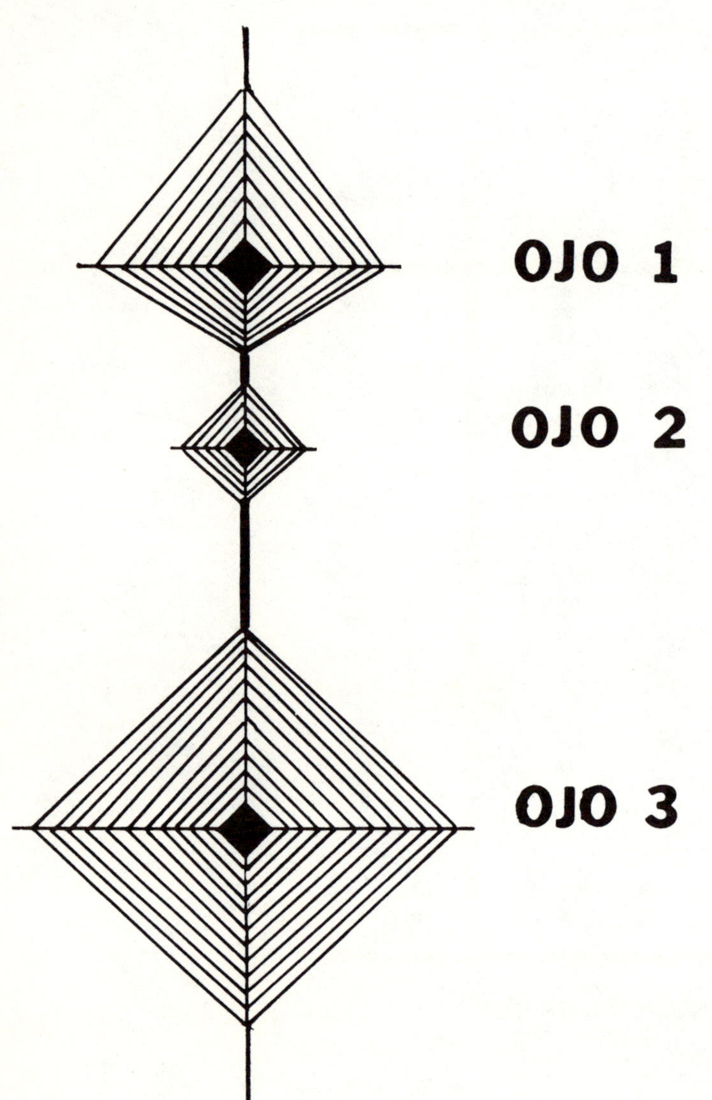

OJO THREE

With color 11, do a 1" double eye

Working a top wrap first on the front, then taking a half turn on arm 1, working a top wrap on back side, and at the same time doing a space wrap by taking two turns on arms 2, 3, and 4, do 4 rounds of color 9.

Continuing with this wrapping do 3 rounds of color 8, 2 rounds of color 12, and 2 rounds of color 10.

Eliminating the space wrap, return to regular double wrapping with color 2 for 4 rounds.

Before gluing off, extend wrap exposed stick to meet ojo number two.

OJO TWO

Always glue off and on on arm 1.

With color 10, make a 1" double eye
With color 7, outline with 1 double round
With color 8 do 1 double round
With color 2, do a single top wrap taking only ½ turn on arm 1, bringing yarn to back side, and top wrap 1 round. (This is because it is not possible to make a single round using double wrap).

With color 11, do 1 double round
With color 2, do a single top wrap on both sides.

OJO ONE

This ojo is double wrapped (See ADVANCED TERMINOLOGY) throughout. Be sure to complete last round on back side before gluing off.

With color 8, do a 1" double eye (See TERMINOLOGY).
With color 13, do 4 rounds
With color 10, do 6 rounds
With color 2, do 2 rounds
With color 11, do 4 rounds
With color 9, do 4 rounds
With color 12, do 2 rounds
With color 8, do 4 rounds
With color 2, do 3 rounds

ROOM DIVIDER

FINISHING:

Using small oblong beads, glue one bead on each arm
of each pinwheel.

Stain six 5" long skewer sticks to match base. Insert in
holes of upper center stick. Trim each end by gluing on
matching oblong beads.

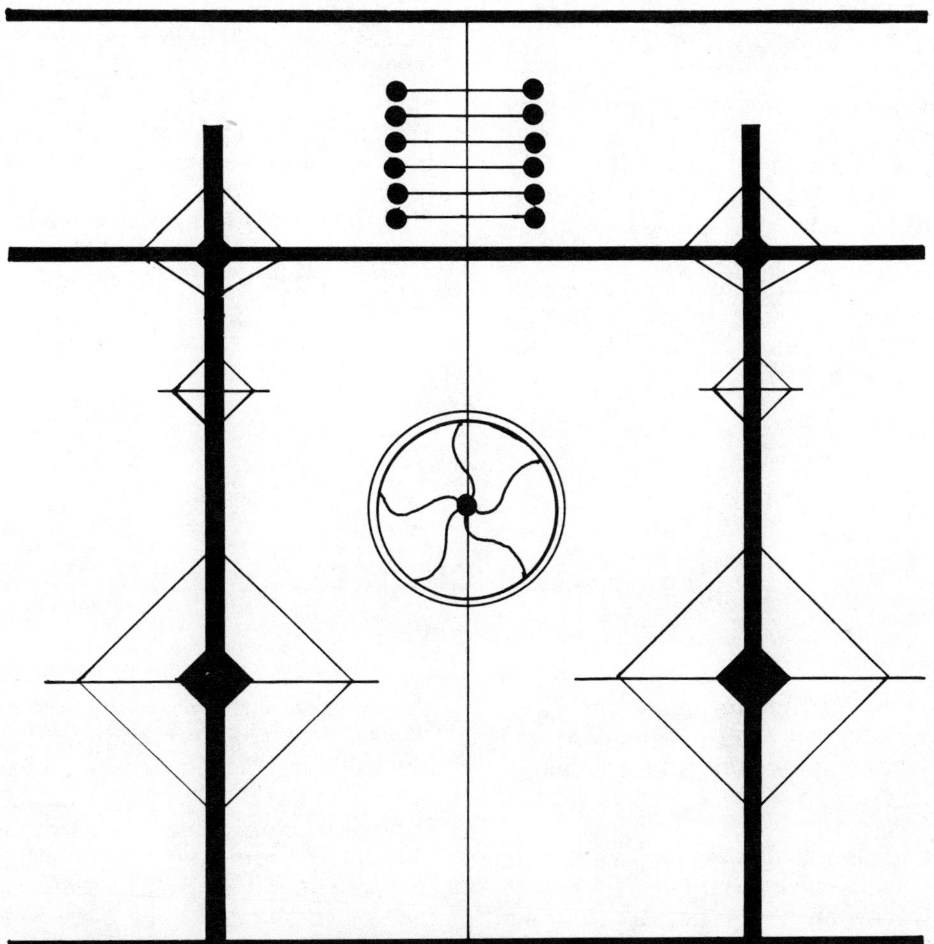

MASTER COLOR CHART
1. Moss green Wintuk or similar lightweight
   yarn
2. Unger #9 in shades of yellow or similar
   bouclé type yarn
3. Light orange Wintuk
4. Light green sport yarn
5. Gold Wintuk
6. Bucilla multi in shades of yellow, orange,
   white
7. Gold Lily Sheen
8. Moss green Lily Sheen
9. Yellow Lily Sheen
10. Orange Lily Sheen
11. Brown Lily Sheen
12. Medium green Lily Sheen
13. Ivory Lily Sheen

YARN SUBSTITUTES

Ojos may be made of almost any thread-like material. If you live in a farming area, try weaving long strands of green hay around a basic ojo frame. When dry the sweet-smelling ojo will act as a closet freshener.

Any type of yarn — orlons, wools, mixtures — may be used. Since the stretch-factor of blends varies, you may have to adjust tension when wrapping with two or more different types of yarns in one ojo.

Silk raffia comes in lovely colors and makes an effective ojo; however, you must be careful of the tendency to vary from lying flat to twisting into a rope. This makes spacing uneven, so either twist firmly as you wind, or be careful to flatten the strands.

Jute may be used, but the resulting ojo will be somewhat bulky in appearance, and jute tends to change tension with atmospheric changes and may sag. Each wind should be anchored with glue.

Ojos may be any size. In **The Creative Ojo Book** very tiny ojos were used to trim a table tree. These were made from the square cross of 1" hardware cloth available in lumber yards. Jewelry ojos were made from corsage pins, gluing 4 together to make the basic ojo frame and using the pearl heads as end trims. Package ties were suggested using toothpick frames. Slightly larger ones may be made of bar-b-q skewers or fireplace matches cut to size. Coffee stirrers or popsicle sticks make slightly larger ojos for us as package ties or tree trims.

Tree trims are most attractive when wound of tinsel ribbon, metallic braids, etc. All these items may be bought in mill end or craft shops. The ojos can be trimmed with miniature figures available in craft shops. It's a nice surprise to receive one of these on a package for they can be added to tree decorations and be used from year to year.

COLOR CHOICES

While the traditional Indian ojos are made in earth colors — brown, gray, black, red, white — modern day ojos are woven in a variety of colors and shades of colors.

The eye is usually dark, signifying the pupil, although some tribes use white signifying innocence. The Mayan Indians will never use yellow in the eye because to them yellow means South and that is the direction of the dead.

This belief is traced to the fact that the sun goes South in the winter and winter was a time of many deaths.

The pyramid on the back of a U. S. dollar bill is topped with an eye. The Egyptians, whose god was Amen Ra, the sun god, considered yellow a lucky color and evidences have been found of a type of ojo used by the Egyptians to please their sun god, painted with a yellow or orange center.

While some ojos are most effective in two or three colors, many designs, such as **3 MASTER** or **NORDISKA**, lend themselves to the use of at least 10 shades. If you want an ojo to pick up the colors in a carpet, drape or bedspread, match your yarns to the colors, and then add a contrasting one.

Unlike other arts, the choice of colors in an ojo is not limited. You will find, however, the ojo demands at least one brilliant color in its execution.

Sometimes the choice of yarns depends on the colors available. There are many more shades of orlon yarns than are found in wools. Blends, orlons, or pure wools may be combined in one ojo when desired colors cannot be found in one kind of yarn. The use of different yarns demands careful attention to tension, but presents no real problem in the finished ojo.

The color used in painting your sticks may either contrast or match the yarn used for the last outside wrap.

Yarn Used: Any type of wrapping may be used — wool, orlon, mixtures, mohairs, rug yarn. In using linens, hemp, or other unusual wraps, tension may be a problem. Small ojos may use single strand or one-ply yarns, tapestry yarns or silk buttonhole twist. Ojos intended for outdoor patio use should be made of nylon yarns which are very difficult to wrap and entail the use of gluing each round in place.

DESIGNING AN OJO

Once you have mastered the basic wrappings and trimmings of an ojo, designing your own ojo to fit a special place or complement a special decor is easy.

The tools required for designing an ojo are inexpensive and easily obtainable. You can buy a square template, a circle template, a protractor, a T-square, a triangle all for a few cents at a variety store.

Because they are made of crossed sticks, all ojos are a variation of a square, a circle, a triangle or a diamond shape. By wrapping extra turns, the ojo may be made to assume a long look in any one direction. By weaving in extra sticks, as in the shield designs, the square ojo can be given a circular appearance.

Start by measuring the space you want to use. Draw a proportionate line on a piece of paper. Then try sketching in the shape you would like to have, using the square template for diamond shapes, squares, kite shapes or tree shapes. Use the circle template to represent shield shapes. Use your angle template to make odd angle designs. Color the sketch, if you want to, with inexpensive colored pencils. Erase and change until you get what you want.

Using basic mathematics, you can figure the proportionate lengths of the sticks you will use, or you may use a slide rule, also available in variety stores.

One caution: All changes in dimension must be in proportion. Thus if you decide to make one of the ojos in this book in a smaller size, don't make the mistake of thinking because you take 6" off the length of the center stick you also take 6" off the other length sticks. You must figure proportion by the formula A:B as X:C. With A as the known length of the stick in the directions, and B as the desired length, X is the unknown length of the cross stick and C is the known length of the cross stick in the directions. By multiplying A and C, and dividing by B, you will find the length you need for the new cross stick. The same formula is used in enlarging the pattern.

In an original design, any combination of wraps may be used to give the ojo your own interpretation. The ojo is as personal as you make it.

EQUIPMENT FOR DESIGNING

Essential Items	Optional Items
Circle Template	Compass
Square Template	T-square
Triangle	Slide Rule
Ruler	French Curve Template
Protractor	Colored pencils
Quadrille-lined paper	Drafting board

HELPFUL HINTS

If you have trouble figuring out your color scheme, cut 1" pieces of your yarn and glue the ends to a small strip of cardboard. You can rearrange the colors for the entire wrapping of the ojo in this fashion.

Unless you wish a very formal ojo, do not use the colors in the same rotation throughout the ojo wrapping. Change their sequence for variety.

Also, do not use the same number of wrappings for every section of color, except when you are matching wing wraps, or directions specify need to match.

You may make an ojo of nothing but top wrap throughout; you may even top wrap a practice ojo all in a variegated wool. This is a good way to learn tension before attempting the more advanced ojos.

In trying out a new design, or in deciding whether you like a combination of wraps, make a small scale ojo. It will let you see what the finished ojo will look like, and you can use the scale model for a package trim.

In mailing ojos for gifts, wrap them securely in corrugated board pieces cut from shipping containers. Wrap in both directions, then do your outside wrapping for mailing. If you are using feathers, take a stitch through the center of the ojo in both directions with a large tapestry needle and attach with a cross of threads to the bottom cardboard. This will keep it from shifting and breaking the feathers.

To keep your ojo fresh, spray liberally with a protective coating such as Scotchguard. Do not try to vacuum your ojo, instead brush it lightly with a lampshade brush, or use your hairdryer to blow air through the threads to remove dust.

If you cannot decide what color you would like to paint your sticks before you start to wrap, wait until you are within the last ½" of wrapping, then carefully paint as close to the yarn as possible, and finish off with your last color.

Counterweights: When making multi-dimensional ojos such as NIGHT OWL, it is necessary to counterweight the ojo to have it hang level. These lead counterweights are available at small cost at any hobby shop carrying model railroad items. They have a self-adhesive backing, and you will put them opposite the end which tends to swing down. Stick them to the back of the sticks, or hide inside the wrapping along the top of a stick on tree-shaped ojos.

When doing a star wrap as a final end wrap, it is not possible to wind feathers into the last turns. In this case, (See HOPI PETAL SHIELD) finish the ojo, then with a pointed tool such as an ice pick, carefully lift threads through the center of the point and slip the quill of the feather which has been moistened with glue, under the threads.

When hanging an ojo from the ceiling (they may also be hung on brackets from walls) staple a thread in place with a paper stapler and fasten to top loop of mobile. Then if you wish to move it, you need not cut the ojo loop. Threads such as crystal sewing thread are practically invisible and the ojo will seem to float in the air.

Any regular ojo may be hung as a mobile by simply attaching a small screw eye in the top arm, attaching a small jump ring and attaching this to the small fishing swivels you can buy in any sporting goods or hardware store. But you must remember to double-wrap any ojo intended to be hung as a mobile so it will be finished on both sides.